Email Marketing in a Digital World

Email Marketing in a Digital World

The Basics and Beyond

Richard C. Hanna
Scott D. Swain
Jason Smith

 BUSINESS EXPERT PRESS

Email Marketing in a Digital World: The Basics and Beyond

First published in 2016 by
Business Expert Press, LLC
222 East 46th Street, New York, NY 10017
www.businessexpertpress.com

ISBN-13: 978-1-60649-992-4 (paperback)
ISBN-13: 978-1-60649-993-1 (e-book)

Business Expert Press Digital and Social Media Marketing and Advertising Collection

Collection ISSN: 2333-8822 (print)
Collection ISSN: 2333-8830 (electronic)

Cover and interior design by S4Carlisle Publishing Services Private Ltd., Chennai, India

First edition: 2016

10 9 8 7 6 5 4 3 2 1

Printed in the United States of America.

Abstract

Despite annual predictions of its demise, email marketing remains one of the most important tools for businesses and other organizations. The reason is simple. Other communication tools, including the collective proliferation of social and digital media channels, cannot duplicate or recreate the unique capabilities of email marketing. And do not let the name fool you—email marketing is not just for marketers. It is for anyone who can imagine the value of being able to reach specific people (and only those specific people) in a timely manner with messages and propositions while also having the ability to directly measure their responsiveness and reactions. This book is intended for those who wish to learn more about how email marketing works, whether as students, teachers, or practitioners. We begin with a recap of the history of email and email marketing and explain how it informs email today. We then cover the fundamentals of email marketing, including types of emails, the elements of an email, email metrics, best practices for email for improving performance, list development, and the benefits of segmenting an email list. Thereafter, we examine special topics to help managers address special needs in email strategy, including the personalities of email recipients, how to run a proper A/B test for optimizing email elements, integrating email with social media efforts, and aligning email with data sources and CRM opportunities.

Keywords

Email marketing, email metrics, email history, CAN-SPAM, A/B testing, social media, email lists, segmentation, big data

Contents

Acknowledgments

We would like to acknowledge those who helped with the completion of this book. Thank you to Rachel Sherman, Lynne Bishop, Forest Davidson, and Scott Donchak for their thoughtful comments, feedback, and overall contributions to early drafts of this book.

The authors would also like to thank BEP for their interest and expertise in bringing this book into being. Special thanks go out to Victoria Crittenden, editor of the digital and social media marketing and advertising collection, and Professor and chair of the marketing division, Babson College, for her vision and support throughout the entire process.

Finally, the authors would like to thank their respective families for their unconditional support and encouragement during the writing of this book.

CHAPTER 1

Email Still Matters

In the words of one senior marketer: "Email marketing is a license to print money." Despite the rise of social and digital media, the evidence is clear—email marketing has capabilities that its alternatives simply do not. In a 2014 survey of 300 U.S. digital marketers, Gigaom Research (underwritten by Extole) found that email marketing was cited as the most effective digital marketing channel for customer retention in the United States, with social network marketing coming in a distant second. Additionally, a 2012 study sponsored by *BtoB Magazine* reported that 59 percent of B2B marketers say email is the most effective channel for generating revenue and that 49 percent of B2B marketers spend more time and resources on email than on any other channel.

This book will teach you how email marketing works. Our approach is different—whereas other books focus on low-level features of email construction and/or tips and tricks for growing an email list, we take a more strategic and theory-driven arc. We examine issues such as the personalities of email users, how email should be integrated with social media activities, the advantages of automating email and connecting it with buyer behavior, and how to run a proper email marketing experiment. But before we get started, let us review some of the reasons why email continues to be the dominant tool in digital marketing.

Why Does Email Continue to Dominate?

Georgia Aquariums, with the help of Silverpop Digital Marketing services (an IBM company), increased their email revenues by 60 percent in two years just by increasing the relevant content they send to their membership via email. Similarly, SmartPak Equine, an online provider of horse supplies and equine supplements, enhanced their email activity by adding automation and integrating customer behavior, and as a result saw a 50 percent increase in conversion rates.

Simply put, email remains the most effective way to target and communicate a *direct* message to a *specified* individual.

- *Email allows one-to-one communication:* Email is similar to sending a direct mail advertisement to a customer's house. As a business, you can target individuals or meaningful groups and be sure that the message was received (but you cannot be sure it was read). In contrast, social media is like dropping a stack of pamphlets over a town and hoping people pass the advertisements out to their friends and neighbors. This approach does not generally result in very precise targeting. Additionally, initial targets in social media will only pass along direct mail pieces if they are excited about your business.
- *Email converts browsers into buyers:* The directness of email can prompt people to make a transition from search or deliberation mode into decision-making mode. Email can move people to action because it presents a direct and immediate marketing message. Such directness is not as efficient with other communication channels such as print mail or other digital media.
- *High return on investment (ROI):* Email marketing is very inexpensive compared to its alternatives. According to a 2015 personalities of email users report by the Direct Marketing Association, the median ROI for email marketing is 21 to 23 percent followed by telephone (19 to 21 percent) and other familiar media (see Figure 1.1).
- *Email reaches a mobile audience:* Email is among the most used mobile applications. Further, individuals often access email more frequently on a mobile device than on a nonmobile device. For example, Justine Jordan at Litmus reveals that "A whopping 66 percent of Gmail opens occur on mobile devices, with only 19 percent opened in a web browser. The remaining 15 percent of Gmail opens occur on desktop email clients."

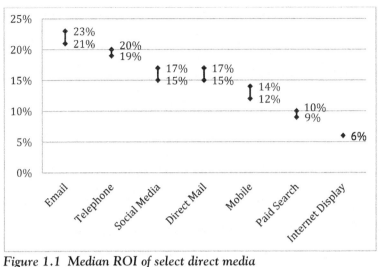

Figure 1.1 Median ROI of select direct media

Source: Direct Marketing Association from an April 2015 study based on a sample of 485 industry responses.

- *Easily measurable:* Email marketing has matured to the point that there are established metrics for assessing the efficiency and efficacy of individual emails and email campaigns. Examples of email metrics include the following:
  - *Opens:* How many people on your list opened the email? This does not mean they read it; this just means that it was not deleted before being displayed.
  - *Clicks:* How many people clicked on an element in the email to get more information or take action?
  - *Click through rate (CTR):* CTR is defined as the number of clicks divided by the number of opens. It is important to note that the CTR is not the clicks divided by total list size (doing so would underestimate the effectiveness of the items of interest since the quality and reliability of lists is imperfect and varies over time).

Addicted to Email?

Of course, email is not just a communication tool used by marketers. Rather, it is *the* most pervasive communication tool used by almost everyone, every day, throughout the day. It may even be fair to say that many people are addicted to email. According to the Relevancy Group, 53 percent of U.S. consumers check their email multiple times per day and 13 percent check hourly or more (see Figure 1.2). You may find it alarming, but a 2012 study of 503 U.S. workers (conducted by Opinion Matters on behalf of GFI Software) found that 59 percent of people check their work email while on vacation and at least 6 percent have checked their work email at a funeral (see Figure 1.3)!

According to a 2013 report published by the Radicati Group, the number of worldwide email accounts is expected to increase from 3.9 billion accounts in 2013 to over 4.9 billion accounts by the end of 2017. Roughly three-quarters of those emails are consumer accounts versus business accounts. Interestingly, the report also indicates that the majority of email traffic comes from business email, to the tune of over 100 billion emails *per day*. From May to June 2013, ReturnPath (an email intelligence company) analyzed the many billions of messages targeted at their panel of 3 million email users, and found that each person received an average of 416 commercial emails per month! And yet, people do not seem to particularly mind. According to a 2015 national survey of 2,057 U.S. adults (conducted by MarketingSherpa), "72 percent U.S. adults prefer companies to communicate with them via email, followed by postal mail (48 percent), TV ads (34 percent), print media (e.g., newspapers, magazines) (31 percent), text message (19 percent), and social media and in-person conversation/consultation (both at 17 percent)."

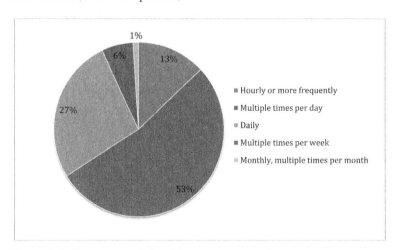

Figure 1.2 Frequency of checking primary email account

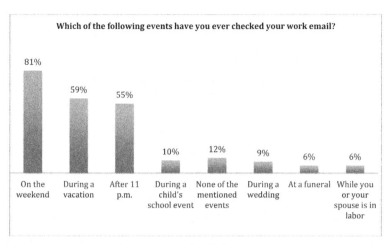

Figure 1.3 Events where people check their email

Of course, there are some caveats as to who checks all of these emails and when they check them. For instance, according to the GFI study, sales, media, and marketing professionals are more likely to check their email on vacation and are never likely to check at a funeral. In contrast, professionals in IT, telecommunications, and finance are likely to check at a funeral. The deeper insight is that predicting whether or when someone will check an email requires an understanding of non-email factors such as how the person manages work–life boundaries, which itself may vary depending on the work environment, organizational culture, the person's personality, and more.

Today, most managers are worried about the time their employees spend on social networks, but the bigger killer to productivity may still be email! According to a 2007 article in the *New York Times*, an observed group of Microsoft workers took, on average, 15 minutes to return to serious mental tasks, such as writing reports or computer code, after dealing with incoming email. While checking their email, they also strayed to reply to other messages or browse the web. Writing for IT Business Edge in 2008, Tom Pisello calculated that the annual, per-person loss of productivity costs organizations approximately $1,250 in time spent dealing with spam, $1,800 in unnecessary emails from coworkers, and $2,100 to $4,100 due to poorly written communications.

Let's Clarify What We Are Talking About in Terms of Commercial Email Senders

Before we go any further, it is important to think about how email senders differ with respect to the nature of their email enterprise. There are two key dimensions we can consider: the purpose of the email and the sophistication of segmentation (see Figure 1.4). With respect to purpose, most emails can be classified as an effort to educate or to convert recipients. Education-oriented emails are about spreading information, directing recipients to other informational content, sharing opinions, or providing some other type of educational value. Conversion-oriented emails are trying to drive traffic with a specific call to action, such as making a purchase of a new item or a sale item, signing up to participate in a conference or webinar, etc. With respect to sophistication of segmentation, emails can be classified in terms of whether they are targeted based on multivariate behavioral customer data and predictive models, versus being untargeted or only coarsely targeted with rudimentary information such as broad geographic location.

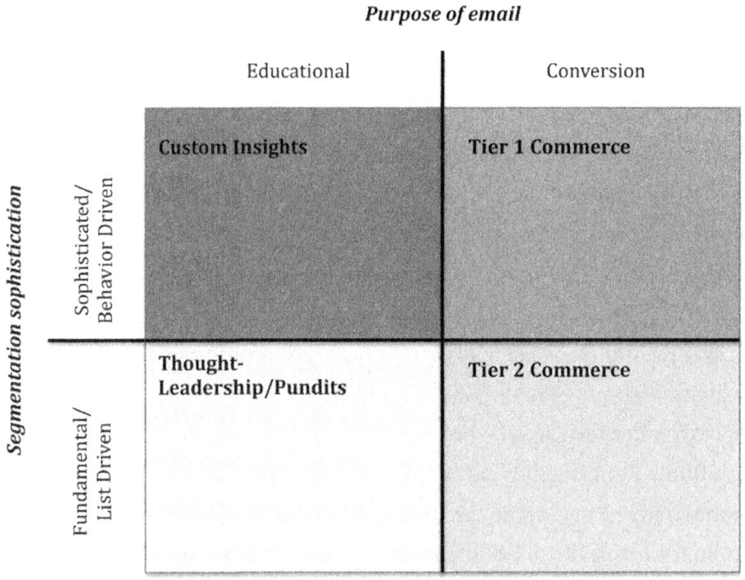

Figure 1.4 Types of email senders

Thinking about the two dimensions simultaneously, we arrive at a 2 × 2 scheme that is useful for identifying four main types of email senders in the ecosystem of email marketing.

- *Tier 1 Commerce (Behavioral data-driven):* Emailers are conversion-oriented and rely on fully automated programs assembled according to user segments described by 100+ attributes of segmentation. Their emails are often personalized and triggered by real-time interactions in physical stores or on websites or apps. Examples of Tier 1 emailers include the largest retailers such as Amazon, Hilton, Target, and Pepsi, all of whom engage in massive, data-driven email campaign enterprises. Tier 1 emailers must design emails in terms of general "creative themes" since there may be hundreds of dynamically created variations.

- *Tier 2 commerce (Basic list-driven):* Emailers are similar to Tier 1 commerce emailers except that their user segments are more predetermined and there are not any active, real-time, or automated triggers. In this case, think: "Let's send an email to people who have been on the website in the last 6 weeks who looked at pet products." The email may still include rich or personalized elements such as a name or a reference to a prior activity.

- *Custom insight:* Emailers are more education- versus conversion-oriented. They use email as a means of distributing custom insights that are tailored to the specific informational needs of their users. The custom nature of the content requires sophisticated user segmentation, which increases its impact on intended users but limits its usefulness for cultivating new customers who may have distinct informational needs (e.g., service-driven businesses such as research firms and large consultancies).

- *Thought-leadership:* Emailers are similar to custom insight emailers except that for them email is a way to establish a reputation for broader thought-leadership through timely articles and other forms of commentary. Since the content is intended to address broad audiences, thought-leadership emailers do not require sophisticated user segmentation schemes or databases. Less effective (but often used) content can also include internal firm news or event content. In this case, list building becomes very important. The concept is to use thought-leadership to cultivate perceptions of expertise and trust among an audience of potential customers (e.g., service-driven businesses such as law firms, accounting firms, or creative services).

- *Pundit:* Emailers are similar to thought-leadership emailers, but rather than representing a business organization, these emailers tend to be individuals. By providing interesting ideas, insights, or curated content, pundits ultimately hope to leverage their credibility to earn ad sponsors or entice their audience to purchase some of their products or services.

- *Teacher:* Emailers are similar to thought-leadership and pundit emailers but possess a more "pure" educational motivation. That is, the mission of these emailers is helping as many users learn rather than seeking to turn a profit from email communications. Some examples would be the Pew Research Centers, NASA, and National Geographic.

Five Fundamental Requirements for Sustained Email Success

As you read this book, five fundamental requirements for sustained email marketing success will emerge:

1. *Make it personal by being relevant:* A "relevant" email is one that is applicable to your audience. Because email allows for one-to-one personalization, there is really no reason that companies cannot send a specific email to different types of customers. If you are not sending relevant emails, eventually your recipients are going to ignore your emails or even unsubscribe. Knowing your customer and what they

interested in is the key to being relevant. Thus, where and when possible, take the opportunity to customize your emails with personal information. Batch-emails that are not personal or identify the individual by name miss a golden opportunity to create a relationship with the buyer and heightening their engagement with the company.

2. *Pay attention to the metrics:* Companies need to pay attention to established email marketing metrics and make adjustments. You will know the value and ROI of your email campaign with the right metrics and also know how to optimize what is working and not working. We will discuss those metrics in the next chapter.

3. *Earn the right to send an email:* Consumers today are inundated with emails. Given that nearly half of emails are examined on a mobile device, the likelihood of an email being deleted without much consideration is high. Therefore, make sure you are a trusted source to the recipient by earning the right to email them through their own opting in.

4. *Coordinate with other channels:* Email should be coordinated with other marketing channels. This means coordinating the message the customer sees across different channels such as social media and traditional media.

5. *Continually collect and use data to optimize emails:* Take advantage of one-to-one connection that email provides. A firm that can (continually) collect data about their customers has an opportunity to use that information to optimize who to send an email to, what to include in that email, and just the right time to send it.

One challenge with personalizing and staying relevant in email marketing is that it requires behavioral data from your customers and matching it with your email activity. Many low-cost email service providers do not have the ability to match that data and instead only provide batch and blast email capability, and cannot provide behaviorally driven targeting for campaigns. The level of sophistication that a company wants to use, will dictate either what type of software they need to have internally or what type of firm they will need to partner with externally. (Something we will address briefly in Chapters 6 and 10).

What Is in This Book?

Here is what you can expect on the rest of our journey through email marketing. The book is divided into three parts. In Part 1, we focus on the fundamentals of email as a tool. To do this, in Chapter 2, we will first examine the roots of email by stepping into the "way back" machine and tracing the historical arc of email technology and usage. The purpose of this is to understand how email has coevolved with other technologies so that we can gain insight into where it may be headed in the future and how it may be integrated with other marketing tools. The next two chapters focus on the basics of email marketing—the concepts and metrics that everyone needs to know. Specifically, in Chapter 3, we examine the anatomy of an email, including a discussion of the common elements, how email works from a process standpoint, and some of technical aspects that email designers have to manage. We will also talk about everybody's favorite nonfood, spam, and cover some of the rules that every email marketer should follow when building a marketing email. Then, in Chapter 4, we examine how email performance is tracked and the key metrics used to evaluate email campaigns and suggest how they can be used to enhance future emails. We also offer suggestions for best practices to improve email performance.

We next move into Part 2 of the book where we delve into the strategies of email marketing. First, in Chapter 5, we will discuss the consumer decision model and buying funnel, and examine how emails can be effectively used at different stages of the consumer purchase process. We will also present some examples of different types of emails commonly used. In Chapter 6, we will address how companies can build an email list and why it is important. Indeed, the Direct Marketing Association finds that emails sent to a company's own "house" list of emails are twice as likely to be opened compared to a rented prospect list. We will also discuss the benefits of segmentation and targeting as well as discuss the difference between email "blasts" and targeted emails. Then, in Chapter 7, we will address a critical component of creating effective emails, namely A/B Testing (where the letters "A/B" prototypically refer to displaying either version A or version B of a test stimulus). A/B testing is a form of experimentation that is crucial for optimizing email marketing. However, many, if not most, companies are not getting A/B testing right because they are focusing on the mechanics of the tests rather than ensuring the validity of the tests.

Finally, in Part 3 of the book, we present topics that go beyond the basics of email marketing strategy. First, in Chapter 8, we will take a closer look at how people interact with email as a technology. Specifically, we consider how peoples' personalities, devices, and work–life environments shape their orientation toward email communication. This is an important foundation for improving current approaches to list segmentation and for recognizing that two people who respond in the same way to email marketing may nevertheless derive very different meanings from the interaction. Then, in Chapter 9, we discuss where email fits with social media activities and we provide insights into integration strategies. Finally, in Chapter 10, we will discuss the benefits of using customer data to optimize email results and explain why most companies are currently unable to do this.

Why This Book?

Email is not going away and thus neither is email marketing. However, there are still challenges for companies who wish to optimize the use of email as well as integrate it with other digital and traditional media technologies. According to a 2012 benchmarking survey by MarketingSherpa, the top five challenges for email marketers are the following:

1. Improving deliverability
2. Using email for funnel optimization
3. Achieving measurable ROI
4. Growing and retaining subscribers
5. Integrating email data with other data systems

Challenges like these are solvable puzzles. However, not everyone is equipped with the knowledge or mental models necessary to devise and implement solutions. Although this book may not provide every technical detail, we believe it provides the necessary foundation to help marketers navigate these five challenges and more.

CHAPTER 2

You've Got Mail! A Trip Down Memory Lane

When and why do you use email? For many people, email is how we communicate and share information between colleagues and friends. As we discussed in the previous chapter, email has become so engrained in our daily lives that most people have probably forgotten how they accomplished anything in a time without email. In the early 1960s there were fewer than 2,000 terminal computers that could send computer-to-computer messages (and all terminals resided in labs at universities). Today, there are over 4 billion email addresses accessed from desktops, tablets, and mobile phones. In just over 50 years, what was originally designed as an efficient way for computer scientists to communicate has become the lifeblood of everyday communication for business and personal use.

In this chapter, we will look back at how these early messages began and the key inflection points that made email accessible, first to larger corporations and government, and later to everyone else. We will also discuss the origin of the term spam and the need for the CAN-SPAM Act of 2003. We will finish with the birth and development of social media and how this phenomenon relates to email marketing.

We Begin at the Beginning

If we think of email as electronic messages, one could argue that the first email was sent via the telegraph over a century ago. However, our more modern conception of email (where we send messages from one computer to another) dates back to the mid-1960s and early 1970s. In the 1960s, computers were enormous machines living in the basements of a few academic institutions and large organizations. Users interacted with the computer (mainframe, see Figure 2.1) through "dummy terminals" (see Figure 2.2). These dummy terminals had no data storage of their own and worked remotely on the mainframe.

Figure 2.1 IBM 7094 Mainframe

Source: http://computer-history.info/Page4.dir/pages/IBM.7090.dir/images/7094.console
.corner.jpg

Figure 2.2 Example of a "dummy terminal"

Source: www-hpc.cea.fr/en/complexe/history.htm

In those days, mainframe computers could not handle more than one operator at a time. Thus, computer users worked in shifts. In 1961, computer scientists at MIT began developing the Compatible Time-Sharing System (CTSS), or the ability for multiple users to use the mainframe computer from different terminals at the same time (Walden and Van Vleck 2011). In 1963, a government agency, Advanced Research Projects Agency (ARPA), funded MIT to further explore mainframe time-sharing, and by 1965 CTSS service allowed up to 30 simultaneous users. As might be expected, the different users needed a way to leave messages for each other regarding different projects or activities they were working on and they would do so using paper notes. Of course, the use of physical mailboxes introduced the risk of messages being lost or ignored due to inconvenience, and alternatives such as voicemail and answering machines had yet to become commercially viable. In 1965, Tom Van Vleck and Noel Morris developed the first email commands to allow users on the same mainframe to leave messages for each other, and thus MAILBOX, one of the first electronic messaging systems, was born.

A few years later on August 30, 1969, the predecessor of the Internet, the Advanced Research Projects Agency Network (ARPANET), came "online" at UCLA. Researchers from Bolt, Beranek, and Newman (formerly BBN, now Raytheon BBN), many of whom had ties to MIT, built the software and hardware that allowed for the first communication over a wired network of two computers at different locations (UCLA and the Stanford Research Institute). Thus began network computing.

Origin of @

Up to this point, messages could be sent only to users on the same computer mainframe. To send messages across a network to a user on a different computer mainframe, some form of "address" was needed to pinpoint a mail location. In 1972, while working for BBN, a contractor for ARPANET, Ray Tomlinson adapted the messaging program SNDMSG to be able to send a message to any computer on the network. He chose the "@" symbol to designate which computer the operator's username lived on. Thus to send a message to a user, one would simply type the person's username followed by the @ symbol and then the name of the mainframe the user was operating. Hence, Ray Tomlinson is often credited as inventing the first electronic message between two computers.

The Late 1970s and the Great Email Debate

Throughout the 1970s and early 1980s, the computer network grew rapidly, and more and more contributors developed common codes and protocols to enhance the utility of computers. Much like open source code communities function today, these programmers were all working on and modifying many of the same computer actions. By the late 1970s, electronic messaging expanded to communicating across different external computer networks, each with its own coding variation. Thus, a critical contribution, similar to the introduction of the "@" symbol, was the introduction of RFC 733 in 1977. RFC 733 resulted from a collaboration of Dave Crocker, John Vittal, Kenneth Pogran, and D. Austin Henderson, and was essentially a specification that called for the standardization of messaging formats across different networks. Hence, when we look at the evolution of email on the computer, we can thank people such as Van Vleck, Crocker, Vittal, and many others for investing and modifying the functionalities we take for granted today.

By the late 1970s, the use of messaging and computers was expanding. In 1976, Queen Elizabeth became the first head of state to send an email (and 29 years later she sends her first tweet!). In the mid- to late 1970s, some of the first commercial, personal computers began to hit the consumer market. For example, the first Apple computer was released in 1976 and the more popular Apple II was introduced around 1978. The use of computers in organizations began to expand, and with it, the need for interoffice communications. This brings us to the origin of the great debate over who invented "email."

In 1978, a 14-year-old computer whiz named (V.A.) Shiva Ayyadurai was challenged to create an interoffice electronic mail system for the University of Medicine and Dentistry of New Jersey (UMDNJ). Ayyadurai ultimately created a system that replicated interoffice paper mail and called it email. He filed an application for copyright in 1982. In recent years, Ayyadurai's claim as the inventor of email has set off a debate about what can be classified as email and who the "true" inventor is. Certainly each contributor during this time period can lay claim to creating some aspect of email, and most of those creations depended on the work that came before them. So, it is hard to say that a single person created email.

Through the late 1970s, computer messaging and email were largely used for communication between programmers and coworkers. However, the way we use email would change in 1978 when Gary Thuerk, a marketing manager at DEC (also known as Digital Equipment Corporation, a major computer company that existed from the 1960s to the 1990s), used the messaging system for something different. Thuerk sent a message to 400 users over the ARPANET, trying to sell a new DEC computer and, as you might expect, received several angry responses. As a result, Thuerk is known as the father of spam. On the flip side, he sold $13 million worth of equipment because of that mailing (Crocker 2012). Although showing early success, the term spam did not become popular until the 1990s and was added to the New Oxford Dictionary in 1998.

During this same time period, Ward Christensen and Randy Seuss developed the first bulletin board systems (BBS), in the midst of the harsh blizzard of 1978 in Chicago. Called the computerized bulletin board system (CBBS), it was the first publicly accessible messaging system. Since it was created before graphical interfaces were available, it is a text-based system (see Figure 2.3). Of course, once the Internet became prevalent and web-based email accessible to all, BBS became less popular. However, BBS are still in use in places where the Internet is less accessible.

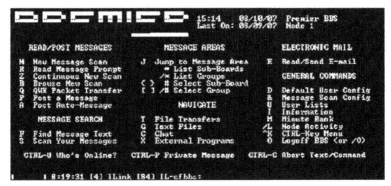

Figure 2.3 Example of a bulletin board system

Source: www.ventureevolved.com/do-not-take-this-software-era-for-granted-pt-2/

With the growth of personal computers from the late 1970s to the mid-1980s, the growth of email technologies came with it. Most of the email systems available during this time were proprietary (e.g., MCI Mail, Telecom Gold, AppleLink) and a user needed to be a subscriber to that system and could send messages only to other subscribers.

The 1980s and the Introduction of SMTP

By 1981, there were four major email networks that connected universities, corporations, and other major institutions: ARPANET (the Internet), UUCP, BITnet, and CSnet (Partridge 2008). Each of the networks had their own communities. For example, CSnet was developed and used by the computer science research community while BITnet was developed by university computing centers to exchange their own information. Although using the "@" symbol was an accepted protocol, what appeared to the left and right of the @ was not standardized across these networks. Thus, an email sender had to know not only which network the receiver was on but also the exact nomenclature for that network. Thus, emails often could be lost or sent to the wrong person altogether.

A critical breakthrough for email came in 1982 with Jon Postel's publication of Simple Mail Transfer Protocol[1] (SMTP). SMTP is a connection-oriented, text-based protocol used to facilitate the sending of emails across different computer networks and servers. It uses a set of codes to simplify how networks communicate and route messages, thus creating a standard for different networks to use and solving the aforementioned addressing problem. Working with a Mail Transfer Agent, SMTP essentially set the rules for how messages would move from one person's computer to a network server and across to another network server, where the message was stored until the receiver picked it up from their computer. Essentially, SMTP is thought of as a store and forward process. Although SMTP has been enhanced since 1982, it remains fundamentally the same today.

Although access to online networks was initially the domain of the military, large academic and research institutions, and large commercial

---

[1] A protocol is an official procedure or a standard method to complete a task that is accepted by everyone.

companies, in the 1980s private companies began to sell access to computer networks to individuals. One of the first online service providers was CompuServe, which launched access to its network services in 1982. CompuServe, formerly known as CompuServe Information Service or CIS, was originally founded to provide computer-processing support to Golden United Life Insurance and operated an independent business in computer time-sharing. However, CompuServe soon recognized potential demand from consumers, and by the early 1990s it became well known by most computer users.

Around this same time in the late 1980s, America Online (AOL) launched its online service to the public. Born from earlier services called Quantum Link (for Commodore computers) and AppleLink (for Apple and Macintosh computers), AOL quickly became popular and is remembered for its announcements, "You've Got Mail!" The cultural meaning of AOL's email service at the time helped inspire the 1998 hit romantic comedy movie *You've Got Mail*, starring Meg Ryan and Tom Hanks (the movie website is still live: http://youvegotmail.warnerbros.com/). When awareness and interest in online services began to take off in the early 1990s, AOL was the major provider of access to homes across the United States. In fact, by 1997, almost half of all U.S. homes that accessed the Internet used AOL (Madrigal 2014). Services such as CompuServe and AOL provided access to forums, online communities, email, games, and other activities. In some ways, these services are the predecessors to social media networks like Facebook and MySpace.

Another evolution in email that began to take shape in the late 1980s was the introduction of email-specific software and organizational products. In 1988, Steve Dorner created Eudora, an email management program that provided one of the first graphical interfaces. This was a free program that was first used primarily with the Macintosh operating system. One year later, the first release of the Lotus Notes email software sold over 35,000 copies (Left 2002). Both of these events marked a new era in how consumers accessed and interacted with email. One particular advantage of a program like Eudora or Lotus Notes was that it offered the ability to filter spam emails and detect fraudulent links. These programs stand as predecessors to Apple Mail, Microsoft Outlook, and others.

The 1990s and the Birth of the Internet as We Know it

Access to the online world quickly changed in the 1990s. In 1991, Tim Berners-Lee (now Sir Timothy, as he was knighted in 2004) and his team at CERN (also known as the European Organization for Nuclear Research, and largest Internet node in Europe at that time) created hypertext transfer protocol (HTTP) and hypertext markup language (HTML), the building blocks for creating and retrieving web pages on the Internet. Essentially, HTTP is a protocol that allows a client (individual computer), using some form of web browser on their computer, to request information from applications living on large computer servers (Internet nodes) and retrieve content in the form of web pages written in hypertext markup language (HTML) along with other files and content. This is the technology that underpins the World Wide Web as we know it today.

The rapid development of the World Wide Web brought changes to email as well. In 1996, Hotmail became the first web-based email service, meaning that consumers no longer had to sign up with proprietary services or closed networks such as America Online or CompuServe. Hotmail was such an immediate hit that Microsoft purchased the company for approximately $400 million in 1997. In the same year, Microsoft also released Outlook, formerly Internet Mail, for the first time.

Of course, with an increase in access to email came an increase in junk email, (i.e., spam). The low (or no cost) benefits of sending an email, compared to traditional postal costs, quickly convinced marketers and businesses of all sorts to follow in the footsteps of Gary Thuerk and send unsolicited emails to thousands of people on the Internet. The first documented use of the term spam occurred in 1993 when Richard Depew attempted to post an item to a user group on Usenet (news.admin.policy), but, due to a software bug, the post repeated itself 200 times. This effectively drowned out any other postings for a period of time. Although in this case it was an accident, drowning out other messages as a practice was not new. In the 1980s, abusive users of message boards, chat rooms, or multiuser dungeon games (the predecessors to World of War Craft) would fill the message space of rivals with lines from a Monty Python skit involving SPAM. In the skit, Viking patrons drown out all other conversations in a café with a song in which they chant "SPAM, SPAM, SPAM," the main ingredient on the café menu (see Figure 2.4). Thus the term spam, or spamming, became symbolic of "something that keeps repeating and repeating to great annoyance" (Internet Society 2014). The Hormel brand, maker of the food item, does not actively object to the use of the word spam in digital contexts but still reserves the right to use the capitalized SPAM for their product.

The first major commercial spam occurred in 1994 when two lawyers began blasting a post on the Usenet to every news group possible to advertise immigration services. Spam posts and emails increased through the late 1990s at an alarming rate, ultimately causing the Federal Trade Commission (FTC) and other organizations to begin hearings on the matter.

Figure 2.4 YouTube clip of Monty Python SPAM

Source: https://youtube/anwy2MPT5RE

The 2000s and Beyond. . .

In the 2000s there were four technology and Internet developments that stand out in relation to email: the CAN-SPAM Act of 2003, the launch of Gmail, the rise of social media, and the introduction of the smartphone.

CAN-SPAM Act of 2003

The CAN-SPAM Act of 2003, signed into law by President George W. Bush on December 16, 2003, is the first national standard for regulating how and when marketers can send commercial emails in the United States. Although the name CAN-SPAM may sound like it refers to the act of canning SPAM, it is actually an acronym for an FCC rules bill sponsored in Congress by Senators Conrad Burns and Ron Wyden called Controlling the Assault of Non-Solicited Pornography And Marketing Act of 2003. The Act establishes the basic rules for sending emails and, more importantly, gives email recipients the right to stop businesses from emailing them. In fact, the CAN-SPAM Act outlines several penalties that can be incurred for violations (though many businesses and recipients remain largely unaware of the rules or penalties).

The actual CAN-SPAM Act makes for difficult reading but fortunately the Federal Trade Commission (FTC) and others have tried to provide "plain language" explanations for businesses (e.g., www.ftc.gov/tips-advice/business-center/guidance/can-spam-act-compliance-guide-business) and consumers (e.g., www.onguardonline.gov/articles/0038-spam). The main requirements for businesses sending emails are as follows:

1. Do not use false or misleading header information.
2. Do not use deceptive subject lines.
3. Identify the message as an ad.
4. Tell recipients where you are located.
5. Tell recipients how to opt out of receiving future email from you.
6. Honor opt-out requests promptly.
7. Monitor what others are doing on your behalf.

What is interesting about these rules is that nowhere does it say a company needs permission to send you a spam email. The key factor is that the email itself has to be clear in what it purports to be or do. Moreover, violation of these rules needs to be reported by the receiver, many of whom are largely unaware of the rules.

Gmail

In 2004, Google launched Gmail on a small scale as an invitation only service. In 2007, Gmail became available to the general public for free. The features that set Gmail apart immediately from its competitors such as Hotmail and Yahoo Mail, were a larger storage capacity for users (1 GB compared to 2 to 4 MB) and a search-oriented, conversation view similar to an Internet forum. Paul Buchheit, the creator of Gmail (and Google's 23rd employee), started the program by building a search engine for his own mail. This search feature became so popular among Google's other employees that Buchheit was asked to create a search engine for everyone's email. Although in today's computer environments, these may seem like small advantages, it must be remembered that, prior to Gmail, storage space was a constant concern and email was not searchable.

Since its inception, Google has continued to innovate the Gmail product, adding threaded conversations, stars and priorities, syncing with calendar, and other software products. One innovation that no longer exists was called Mail Goggles. Yes, it was an allusion to the more familiar notion of "beer goggles." When enabled, Gmail would not allow the user to send an email without first taking a math quiz to make sure the user was in the right "state of mind" to be sending email. Of course, the default time setting for Mail Goggles was late nights on weekends. Sadly, this feature is no longer available.

In the summer of 2012, Gmail surpassed Hotmail in users for the first time to become the largest email service provider in the world, boasting approximately 425 million monthly active users. Today Google competes with Microsoft as an enterprise solution for email and other office software for small to large businesses.

The Rise of Social Media

Social networking started long before the 2000s with BBS and AOL. However, in the late 1990s two of the first social networking sites on the

World Wide Web emerged, Classmates.com and SixDegrees.com. Classmates was about finding friends from a person's high school days, while SixDegrees was based on the concept of six degrees of separation, which holds that any one person is connected to any other person by six or fewer relations. A popular implementation involving movie and television star Kevin Bacon (https://oracleofbacon.org) computes the fewest number of movie links required (i.e., the "Bacon number") to connect Kevin Bacon to any given actor or actress. Neither of these early social networks was able to sustain themselves (though Kevin Bacon resurrected the namesake as a nonprofit in 2007 in the form of SixDegrees.org: www.sixdegrees .org), but the idea of what they provided lives on in the next wave of social media. In 2002, Friendster.com built on the SixDegrees concept of inviting your friends to connect. In 2003, LinkedIn extended the classmates concept of linking people by a shared experience, but making it a professional network by connecting people through work affiliations. These launches were quickly followed by MySpace in 2003, Facebook in 2004, Twitter in 2006, and now many others.

Social media networks make connecting with people from afar easier and more organized as well as making it easier to share rich media. As people turned to social media to connect with each other, businesses followed them by launching their own brand pages in Facebook or establishing Twitter accounts to broadcast their latest deals and product launches. As a result, much like the conversations around the death of the postal service in the late 1990s (and even today), the conversation in the 2000s began to shift to whether social media would be the death of email.

The Introduction of the Smartphone and Mobile

The evolution of smartphones in the early 2000s facilitated a major shift in the way people used email and other software to communicate. Smartphones in the 1990s (e.g., IBM Simon or the Nokia 9000 Communicator) were bulky devices with limited memory and capabilities—though widely popular because they offered something more than the standard mobile phone. In the early 2000s, smartphones began to combine the functionality of a Personal Digital Assistant (PDA) with a mobile phone in a smaller frame. The screens were monochrome and allowed for simple, installable software. However, most of the activity was still text-based.

The launch of the Blackberry changed the way professionals did business. The device had a full QWERTY keyboard and made responding to email and other quick messages on the go more viable than before. The market was abruptly changed again in 2007 with the launch of the first iPhone by Apple, Inc. It introduced the first touch screen, provided an Internet experience that mirrored a user's experience on the computer, and created the "there's an app for that" mentality. The introduction of the iPhone was significant for both email and social media because it allowed people to have access to these activities around the clock. Instead of being tethered to a computer, people were free to roam and still stay connected to the digital world. As a result, we have seen an increase in email open rates on mobile phones relative to desktop open rates. Mobile marketing is on the rise, while traditional marketing struggles to hold a place in consumers' lives. Today, email marketers must not only consider the message they want to deliver but also the environment in which the recipient consumes it. This is a topic we will address in more detail later in the book.

As you can see, while email has a long history (see Figure 2.5), the process and technology of email has not changed significantly since its inception. However, the sheer volume of emails we engage with, the advancement of computers and the ability to use rich media, along with the competing noise of other technologies (e.g., social media, smartphones) has changed how we interact with email.

Exercise: Where Were You When You First Emailed?

Thought exercise: Read the questions below and jot down some notes.

Think back to your first experience with email. How old were you? Who did you email and why? What did you use to send your email? Where were you in the timeline discussed in this chapter? Now fast forward to today. How often do you use email? How many emails do you get in a day? How important is email to your daily routine?

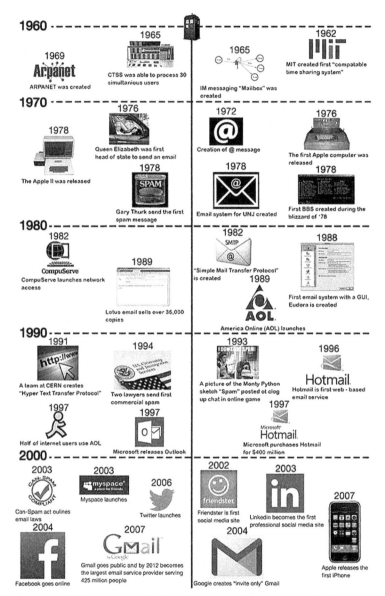

Figure 2.5 Milestones in the development of computers, the Internet, and email.

References

Crocker, D. (March 20, 2012). *A history of e-mail: Collaboration, innovation and the birth of a system.* Washington, DC: Washington Post.

Internet Society (July, 2014). *The History of Spam: The Timeline of events and notable occurrences in the advance of spam.* Geneva, Switzerland.

Left, S. (March 13, 2002). *Email timeline.* London: The Guardian.

Madrigal, A.C. (December, 2014). *The fall of Facebook: The social network's future dominance is far from assured.* Washington, DC: The Atlantic.

Partridge, C. (2008). "The technical development of internet email," *IEEE Annals of the History of Computing* 30, no. 2, pp. 3–29.

Walden, D. and Van Vleck, T. (2011). *The Compatible Time Sharing System (1961–1973): Fiftieth Anniversary Commemorative Overview,* Washington, DC: IEEE Computer Society.

CHAPTER 3

The Anatomy of an Email and Email Environments

Imagine you are attending a meeting with a group of email marketers, and the topic is how to improve your company's use of email. To understand what everyone is talking about, you have to know the lingo or the vocabulary of email marketing. In this chapter, we will cover the basic design of an email, how an email works, and what technical considerations a sender needs to consider. We will also discuss how email marketers must manage the design of these elements to maintain compliance with the CAN-SPAM Act while also increasing the likelihood of emails being opened and driving clicks.

The Look and Feel of Email

You have probably already opened and written thousands of emails, so you already know what an email looks like. However, we now want to more consciously and mindfully focus on the different parts of an email that marketers need to modify and optimize. There are typically seven key parts of a marketing email (see Figure 3.1):

1. *Send date and time:* Every email has a time and date stamp on when it is sent.
2. *Header:* This section contains the "to" and "from" information for the email. The "from" line contains the email address from which the email was sent. Given the amount of spam and fraudulent emails that are sent out daily, it is critical that the name and the email address shown in the "from" line clearly identify the sender.
3. *Subject line:* This line contains the reason to open the email. Most people will decide whether to open, delete, or save an email based

on the attractiveness of the subject line to their needs combined with the sender's identity.

4. *Primary message:* This is also the primary headline in the body of the email. It should support the message in the subject line.

5. *Body:* The main part of the email, which typically contains images and information.

6. *Call to action:* Often the most important part of the email is the call to action. This is what marketers are hoping the reader will act upon, whether it is "click here to sign up," "learn more," or "buy now."

7. *The footer:* The final element is essentially the "fine print," which includes information about the company sending the email, their physical location, and an option for the recipient to unsubscribe or opt out of the email list.

Figure 3.1 The elements of a marketing email

How marketers implement the last six elements dictate whether the email is in compliance with the CAN-SPAM Act of 2003. The first six elements of the email can make the difference between success and failure of a particular campaign. Thus, a major part of developing a successful campaign is testing different variations of these elements to find the optimal configuration.

Staying in Compliance with CAN-SPAM

Recall from Chapter 2 when we discussed the CAN-SPAM Act of 2003 that there were seven key rules to follow:

1. Do not use false or misleading header information.
2. Do not use deceptive subject lines.
3. Identify the message as an ad.
4. Tell recipients where your company or organization is located.
5. Tell recipients how to opt out of receiving future email from you.
6. Honor opt-out requests promptly.
7. Monitor what other agencies are doing on your behalf.

Companies sending emails can be compliant with CAN-SPAM by designing and sending emails according to the above rules. As you can see in Figure 3.1, the header clearly identifies *Unleashed by Petco* as the firm sending the email. If the recipient clicked on the email of the sender, they would see the specific email address as well. Spammers often disguise the name in the email address with a different title. Similarly, notice the subject line of the email properly matches the body of the email. An unscrupulous sender might use a bait and switch where the subject line is written to entice opening but the body of the email would contain something very different. The body of the email in Figure 3.1 clearly represents itself as an ad for the firm, and the fine print identifies both the location of the firm and a link to opt out of future emails.

In addition, the sending firm is fully compliant if, upon clicking the unsubscribe button, the email recipient is brought immediately to a web page where they can change their subscription options. In some cases, companies will provide a notice that automatically unsubscribes the recipient. In other cases, the company may ask the recipient to verify if they want to unsubscribe first or possibly offer the recipient an option to receive fewer emails or select types emails. Unsubscribe requests provide an opportunity for the company to learn why the recipient is unsubscribing by either providing some multiple choice questions or providing a space for an open-ended response. This knowledge can be used to refine email strategies. Upon receiving an unsubscribe request, the company has ten days to remove the individual from their email list. In other words, if the company sends the recipient another commercial email (not including transactional emails) after the ten days have expired, they are in violation of CAN-SPAM and the recipient is within their rights to report the offending company to the FTC. For most companies, removing a person from a list should take less than 24 hours. A firm is also *not* compliant with CAN-SPAM if they either make this terminating process extra difficult or nearly impossible to complete (e.g., in the hopes that the recipient will give up). Finally, the last item on the CAN-SPAM list specifies that if a company uses a third party to manage their email process, the hiring company is still responsible for their email action completed on their behalf—so all the rules still apply!

The Technical Side: How Emails Work

As mentioned in Chapter 2, emails started as simple text messages between two people and gradually grew to include other functionality we take for granted today, such as multiple receivers, blind copies, forwarding, inclusion of attachments, HTML and images, and many other features. Even today, most emails exchanged between individuals, whether they are friends or work colleagues, are mostly text based. However, the emails marketers use most often take advantage of web programming languages HTML and CSS to add graphics, animations, action buttons, and other advanced formatting to grab customers' attention and nudge them into action. To better understand the challenges that an email designer faces, marketers need to know the vocabulary and understand some of the technical aspects behind email processes and design.

The Three Email Client Environments

Although there are a variety of programs that can be used to access, compose, and send email we classify these programs into three types of email clients[1]: desktop email clients, webmail clients, and mobile email apps. Desktop email clients include Outlook, Apple Mail, Thunderbird, Lotus Notes, Postbox, and several others. Although they have their own special bells and whistles, they all send and receive email the same way and they provide the same basic functionality. Webmail clients include Outlook.com, Gmail.com, Yahoo.com, Hotmail.com, iCloud.com, and others and are essentially web programs that are accessed through a web browser. These webmail clients offer similar functionality as the desktop clients, but perhaps not all of the features. The main benefit is that an individual is not tethered to a single computer to access their mail. Using a web browser, one can access email from any computer with an Internet connection anywhere in the world. Finally, mobile email apps, such as Android Gmail, Apple Mail, Outlook, and others, are designed to specifically work on mobile devices, and although they handle the basic functionality like their desktop brethren, they are generally stripped down of many of the advanced features.

Given the number of people who own smartphones, tablets, and computers, it is very likely that many people use all three in a given day. What the three environments share in common is the process in which email is sent across the Internet. However, both across and within the three environments, several of the email clients have different mechanics that can cause the identical email to appear entirely different. For the typical user that sends a text email with minor formatting and maybe an attachment, this is a nonissue as text emails almost always appear the same. However, for the email marketer who is sending emails with graphics or animation with hyperlinks and other formatting, these three environments pose considerable display issues that have to be accounted for. While an expert design team or a third-party email agency handles or has a work-around for many of the issues that can come up, it is

---

[1] A word of caution: The technical definition of an email client is a computer application used to access, read, and compose emails. However, the term email client is also used to broadly refer to all email programs regardless of environment.

important for marketers to know a little about the mechanics of the email process and how emails appear in these email environments to properly plan their marketing activities.

The Process of Sending and Receiving Email

Every email address has two components, the recipient's identification (e.g., j.t.kirk) and the individual's location on the Internet called the domain address (e.g., @federation.gov). After we compose an email on our computer using a program like Outlook or a webmail client like Gmail and press the "send" button, the program sends the email and any attachments to an outgoing mail server using SMTP (see Figure 3.2). Using the domain address of the recipient, the outgoing mail server searches for the correct IP address and contacts the recipient's receiving mail server to make sure the recipient actually exists there. If the recipient is not valid at that address, then the email is rejected and the sending mail server sends a failure message back to the sender. If the address is valid, the email is then sent to the recipient's domain receiving mail server.

The receiving mail server, also known as a mail transfer agent, accepts the message and then places the email into the recipient's "mailbox" where it is stored. In the 1980s and 1990s, this mailbox had limited storage capacity; however, today, most mail servers can handle an extremely large capacity. Additionally, many Internet service providers and other large companies that manage email exchanges have built a filtering process into the receiving servers that can block emails or automatically direct them into quarantine or a junk folder before the user has accessed them. For example, if a sender is not on an approved list or the email has contents that are identified as problematic, the email can be diverted from a user's mailbox or blocked altogether.

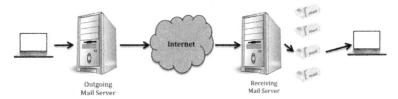

Outgoing Mail Server

Internet

Receiving Mail Server

Figure 3.2 Graphical depiction of how email works

The next time the recipient logs into their mail server, the email client they use will fetch the email from the server mailbox using either Post Office Protocol (POP) or Internet Message Access Protocol (IMAP) processes. When using POP, all of the emails in the mailbox are downloaded to the email program and subsequently deleted in the mailbox. However, when using IMAP, the emails are copied from the mailbox onto the receiving email program. Whatever the user does to the email on their reading program, a message is sent back to the mail server mailbox to update its status. Thus, by using IMAP, one can access their mailbox on the server from multiple places or devices and see the status of their email no matter where and when they are accessing it. Whereas with POP, once the email is downloaded to the email program, it resides in that specific device.

Launch All Emails

One thing that a mass email sender wants to avoid is accidentally exposing their email list to all their recipients. If you put more than one address in the "TO" section, then all of the addresses will be visible. If you hide those names by giving it a group name, then there is a different problem. If one respondent responds to the message with a reply all, everyone in the group will receive the reply. Those issues aside, there are two important reasons why you cannot put multiple addresses in a mass email, regardless of how you place them (i.e., grouped, blind copy, etc.): (1) lack of personalization and (2) inability to track individual response. As we discussed in Chapter 1, a key advantage to email over other types of media is the one-to-one communication email affords you. By sending to a group *en masse*, the sender forgoes that opportunity to personalize. And, as we will address in the next chapter, without a unique email to each individual, actual response cannot be measured. Thus, if you have a list of 1,000 email addresses, 1,000 emails need to be sent. If you have a list of 1,000,000 email addresses, then 1,000,000 emails need to be sent out. (Note: No one hits the send button that many times! Specialized software services can send out thousands of emails simultaneously.)

Message Format: Attachments, HTML, and MIME

Email was originally built as a text-only communications form. So, to send a picture, document, or any other attachment, the file has to be converted to a plain-text format which is then attached to the body of the email. Once the recipient received the email, this plain text code had to be converted back into its file format. This conversion had to be done manually by the recipient until the creation of Multipurpose Internet Mail Extensions (MIME). MIME is built in and works behind the scenes in all email programs and web clients during the process of sending and receiving. If an email is only plain text, MIME is not needed. However, if there is any attachment or HTML formatting, MIME works by first identifying the format being used (i.e., .jpg, .html, .doc, etc.) and whether it is an attachment or built in to the message, then converts it into plain text. Using the information from the initial MIME process, the recipient's email program can then reverse the process to return the file to its original form.

Because of this process, emails should not include embedded files or other images that the email marketer wishes to show up when the email is opened. If image files are embedded, emails will often not render correctly. Instead, emails should be designed to just include HTML (which is just text), and the images should be hosted on a server and "called" by the HTML when the email is open. This process will keep email size small and result in the best-looking emails.

Look back to Figure 3.1 earlier in this chapter. In that particular email, the graphics and buttons you see are not attachments or files embedded in the email. In fact, properly coded commercial emails that have graphics never embed them in the actual email. If they did, there is no guarantee that the graphics would appear in the right place or load at all. Because of the MIME process, these files would be reassembled and then placed as attachments separate from the body of the email instead of included in the body of the email.

Emails today are created similarly to web pages. All of the images, buttons, animations, and others are stored on a web server managed by the sender. The email itself is coded like a web page in that when the email is opened, the code in the email sends a request from that server to download those images. In fact, most commercial email senders bundle the HTML code with a plain-text version of the email, so that if there is a problem with getting the image from the web server, at least the plain-text version will still communicate the message. Unfortunately, the way an email appears, or renders, in the (i.e., desktop email clients, webmail clients, and mobile email apps) can vary greatly.

The biggest concern for email marketing design is how the formatting and graphics will render (i.e., appear) in different email clients and environments. The process is somewhat technical and the complete details are beyond the scope of this book. Typically, these design issues are in the domain of email designers and coders. For those who already have some experience in coding, there are many tips and tools available on the Internet to learn more about the technical side of coding emails. However, many firms and small businesses outsource this process to agencies and specialty firms such as Constant Contact, MailChimp, Litmus, and many others that provide email templates and services. Regardless, anyone planning to be involved in email marketing needs to have a basic understanding of what is happening and the key vocabulary, as well as be aware of the biggest roadblocks to emails rendering the same in every client.

Email Rendering

Every email program, whether it is a desktop client, web-based client, or mobile app, has a rendering engine, which is a software component that takes HTML, XML, images, and others along with any formatting information (e.g., Cascading Style Sheets) and displays the content on the screen according to the instructions in the code. Email clients do not have their own rendering engine and instead typically use one that has been built for other purposes such as web browsers. Herein lies the difficulty: not every email client uses the same rendering engine, which means the identical email will not look the same across different clients.

For example, in 2007, Microsoft changed Outlook's rendering engine from the one used in Internet Explorer to one that is based on Microsoft Word. This rendering engine relies on tables and different coding compared to most rendering engines used in browsers. As a result, emails opened in Outlook might have different colored text, lost background colors, or broken animations. Apple Mail for desktop and mobile devices uses a rendering engine called WebKit, which is the rendering engine in web browsers Safari and Chrome. WebKit is the most versatile and allows an abundance of formatting and style features. Any emails designed specifically for WebKit rendering may run afoul on Outlook. On the other hand, while one might expect Gmail, since it is browser based to render similarly to other browsers, it actually strips out style formats unless it is written in line with the coding, adding an extra step to preparing emails. Luckily, many third-party services such as Mail-Chimp, PutsMail, and Litmus, to name a few, provide tools to help companies create inline styles.

Mobile vs. Computer

Mobile email apps are closely related to email clients with the key difference being that emails appear differently on a mobile device because of the screen size. In a 2013 study sponsored by Facebook, International Data Corporation surveyed 7,446 iPhone and Android users in the United States (18 to 44 years old) over the course of a week and found that email was the single most common activity on smartphones, ahead of web browsing, social media, and games. Further, recently in 2014, Experian reported that 53 percent of all email opens occurred on a mobile phone or tablet.

An immediate challenge in designing "mobile-friendly" email is that the sending server for the email cannot detect the receiving device to send differently formatted messages depending on the device. In contrast, servers *can* detect the receiving device for a web page and serve up a mobile version or a desktop version. This means email marketers must design emails that simultaneously work well on mobile and desktop devices. There are three approaches to consider when addressing how to design for mobile versus desktop apps: agnostic approach, fluid designs, and responsive designs.

The agnostic approach, also referred to as mobile aware or scalable approach, requires designing an email with mobile uses ahead of others. That is, design your layout based on what works on a mobile screen first (i.e., single column, large buttons, short and concise copy) and use that regardless of screen size. Alternatively, a fluid design has the email automatically enlarge or shrink to fit the screen size. The industry standard for email design is to make an email 600 pixels wide. In fluid-designed emails, the width is not fixed, and instead it is set by the percent of the screen you want to use, which in this case would be 100 percent. Thus on smaller screens, the email shrinks to fit, and on larger screens, the email enlarges. The downside of this approach is that text tends to wrap in the wrong places and buttons can get misaligned. The last approach, which is ideal but also more complex, is called responsive design. In responsive designs, the designer sets up conditions in the code that place elements of the email in different places on the screen depending on screen size. So for a small screen, a call-to-action button might appear in the middle of the email, but on a larger screen that button might shift to the right to align with another element. The designer has to create a different look for different screen sizes and build that into code. A media query, which is code written into the email to detect the screen size of the device is the key to responsive emails. However, some mobile apps like Gmail (both IOS and Android), some versions of Windows phone, and older versions of the Android Mail app, do not support media queries, which can be problematic.

If you want to learn more about the coding and design aspect of email, there are many free resources available on the Internet. Also, several of the email service providers such as MailChimp, Litmus, Email on Acid, among others maintain a blog with tips and advice for dealing with a variety of email design challenges. As we will discuss in later chapters, learning about your customers, purchase behaviors as well as device usage can help alleviate many of guessing games and allow marketers to send more effective emails both in terms of content offering and appearance.

Exercise: Evaluate Your Email

Consider the set of commercial emails you have received over the last few days. Can you pick out one that you opened and one that you immediately trashed? For these two emails, do the following:

1. For one day, collect all of the commercial emails that arrive between 12:00am and 11:59pm for one email account. How many did you receive? Did you receive multiple emails from the same sender?

2. Explain your reasoning for opening and trashing, respectively, these two emails.
3. Circle the seven elements discussed earlier in this chapter. To what extent did each of these influence your actions with the email?
4. Now, take the email you trashed. Explain how you could fix this email to increase the chances of opening it in the future.
5. Now, take the email you opened. Explain what you could change to decrease the chances of opening it in the future.

References

Experian. (2014). "Q3 2014 Email Benchmark Report," *Quarterly Email Benchmark Reports*, Experian Marketing Services.
International Data Corporation. (2013). "Always connected: How smartphones and social keep us engaged" (Research Report sponsored by Facebook).

CHAPTER 4

The Metrics of Email Marketing

One of the key benefits of email marketing is that it is highly measurable, and hence it is possible to determine return on investment fairly accurately and precisely. In this chapter, we introduce the established metrics for email marketing, along with some industry benchmarks. We will also recommend best practices to improve email marketing performance on these metrics.

How to Track an Email

Tracking happens in all commercial emails. The main method for tracking email activity is to insert an image that is so small (usually a single pixel, the smallest addressable element on a display device) that it is invisible to the naked eye. Recall, in the previous chapter, we discussed that an HTML email essentially is coded like a web page; hence, when the email is opened, a request is sent to a web server that hosts all the images for the email. For the tracking pixel, when the email is opened, the email-receiving server (where the received email resides) sends a request to the email sender's computer server for the appropriate images saved there. The pixel, being one of those images, is then triggered by this event. When the pixel is sent, the tracking begins.

Contained in the pixel is a unique customer ID. This ID could be an alphanumeric code or the email address. Regardless, it needs to be unique to the receiver so that when the pixel is activated, that code is then sent back to the sender's servers. While this can be done manually, one of the advantages of using a third-party vendor, as discussed in the previous chapter, is that this tracking process is built into their software and simply needs to be activated by the user. In addition to the unique

ID, pixels can be set up to track the receiver's operating system, device, or other information.

A problem with the image pixel technique is that some email programs block all images in an email from opening unless specifically requested by the user. What this means is that the tracking pixel is never loaded and thus never sends back user information even if the recipient browses the email without images. As a result, open rates may be artificially low. In the case of Gmail in the web browser, images are automatically cached, or stored, until the user requests them. Thus, the first, or unique open, can be tracked, regardless of whether individual downloads the images to their computer or not, but subsequent opens of the same email by the same user cannot be tracked unless they download the images.

Measuring Email Performance Through Metrics

There are eight metrics we would like to cover. Each of these metrics tells a story in itself. However, combining more than one metric along with information about user segments tells a more complete story that can cover both campaign performance and the health of an email list. As you will see, a key aspect to any metric is keeping track of the base that it is drawn from. We describe each metric below (see Figure 4.1 for a summary).

Delivery Rate: The percentage of emails that successfully reach a target email account. According to Marketo (2013), delivery rates across industries averaged 95 to 98 percent, with top performers having delivery rates above 98 percent. If your delivery rates are low even after "cleaning" the list by correcting typos and removing "dead" email addresses, there may be other, less obvious, issues that need to be investigated (Shankaranarayanan, Even, and Berger 2015). For example, if emails sent to a particular domain address are all bouncing back, it is likely a new spam filter has been put in place and your emails are wrongly being sent to the trash or being rejected outright. In this case, you may need to contact the customers directly using another method to have your emails put on a safe sender list.

Delivery rate = # emails delivered / Total # sent
Open rate = # emails opened/ Total # delivered
Click thru rate (CTR) = # times link clicked / Total # delivered
Click to open (CTO) = # times link clicked (by recipient) / Total # opens
Conversion = # Purchased/Action (at website)/ Total # delivered
Adjusted conversion = # Purchased/Action (at website)/ Total # click-thru

Figure 4.1 Summary of key email metrics

Bounce Rate: The percentage of emails that do not deliver properly and are returned (i.e., 1 – delivery rate). However, not all bounced emails should be treated the same. We distinguish between two types of bounced emails: soft bounces and hard bounces. A *soft bounce* occurs when an email is undelivered because an individual is on vacation (e.g., autoresponse is activated) or the individual's email box is full. A *hard bounce* occurs when an email is permanently undeliverable because, for example, the email address is typed incorrectly, the email address is invalid, or some other uncorrectable fault.

Soft bounce rates are less of an issue with the email list and more of a timing issue for the specific individuals. Hard bounces speak more to the quality of the list itself. One way to reduce hard bounces due to invalid email addresses or typos is to use a double opt-in approach when collecting email addresses. Moreover, an email address that repeatedly has a soft bounce should be viewed as a hard bounce and removed from the list. As discussed with delivery rates, cleaning an email list regularly should also contribute to reducing hard bounces. If these efforts have minimal impact on hard bounce rates, then it is time to take a closer look at the list-building process.

Open Rates: Number of opened emails (i.e., those that trigger the tracking pixel) divided by the total number of successfully delivered emails. Most marketers like to make a distinction between *unique opens*, or the first time an email is opened, versus *total opens*, the number of times an email is opened including repeat opens. As mentioned earlier, open rates can often be artificially low if the receiver has an image blocker on as default and hence the tracker is never triggered. Similarly, if an image blocker is not on, images can load by simply scrolling through emails in a preview pane, and hence the tracker is triggered even though the recipient does not actually open the email and give it a complete read—thereby potentially inflating open rates as well. Thus this metric by itself has some inherent weaknesses.

According to Marketo, open rates across industries averaged 10 to 15 percent, with top performers having open rates above 16 to 20 percent. To improve open rates, companies should emphasize segmenting and targeting strategies to make sure the sent email is relevant to the recipient. Additionally, companies can reach out to the people on the email list with a formal request to be put on the receiver's approved sender list in their email program so that these emails are trusted and images are less likely to be blocked. Finally, having a subject line that garners interest, along with other images in the email that encourage viewing, will increase the likelihood that the recipient opens the email and triggers the tracker, and of course most importantly, views the message content.

Click-Through Rates (CTR): Number of click-throughs (i.e., clicking on a link or button in the email) divided by the number of emails delivered. However, CTR might be evaluated and treated differently depending on the base. For example, CTR could be the number of click-throughs divided by the total number of emails sent. Alternatively, we might consider only the unique or first clicks by unique opens. Each of these gives a slightly different perspective on the performance of an email. According to Marketo, CTR (based on emails delivered) across industries averages 2.1 to 5 percent, with top performers having CTR in the range of 5 to 10 percent.

CTR can be improved by having a clear and accessible call-to-action link. Format and highlighted content can also influence CTR. It helps, of course, when the call to action is related to the subject line. All of these things can and should be tested by marketers as they are developing their campaigns, which will be discussed in later chapter. Finally, as in any promotion, creating a sense of urgency to act on the call to action is likely to increase CTR. Effective means of enhancing urgency include offering incentives and conveying time limits or deadlines (Hanna, Berger, and Abendroth 2005; Swain, Hanna, and Abendroth 2006).

Click-to-Open Rate (CTO): The number of click-throughs divided by the number of emails opened. The benefit of this metric over CTR is that it removes the impact of low open rates and gives a marketer a sense of the impact of the email for those who truly opened. According to Marketo, CTO rates across industries average 11 to 15 percent, with top performers having CTO rates in the range of 16 to 20 percent.

Conversions: Completing an action of interest to the marketer at the landing page or on the website after clicking through from an email. For example, if Hanes (a basic apparel marketer) sends an email promoting a discount on T-shirts and a person clicks on the call to action in the email and then purchases five T-shirts, it counts as a single conversion (assuming that "purchase" is the ultimate behavior of interest). The value of the total purchase would be considered a separate metric. The same applies if the call to action is to fill out a survey or sign a petition. Each completed survey or petition signature would count as a single conversion. Similar to CTR, the *conversion rate* will vary depending on what base we use. We learn something different depending on whether it is conversions relative to emails delivered or emails opened or even conversion relative to CTR. If it is conversions relative to the number delivered or opened, we have a gauge of the performance of the email. However, knowing conversion relative to CTR or CTO can provide insights on whether the landing page for the clicked link is effective or not. For example, an email promoting a discount on ski helmets at a sporting goods store that links directly to a landing page with the specific helmets on deal displayed and a banner advertising the discount will be more effective than a link that simply brings customers to a general landing page for helmets. If conversions relative to CTR are low, we know we are losing people at the website. If conversions relative to emails sent are low, we have a sense for the campaign, but the conversion rate may be low because of the overall open rate or some other factor.

Average Order Value: The dollar value spent for a purchase/conversion tied to an email. For example, imagine an email from Hanes.com promoting a three-pack of crew neck T-shirts on sale for $15.00. Let us assume there are three purchases: one person buys a three-pack of crew neck T-shirts for $15.00, another person buys a three-pack of crew neck

T-shirts for $15.00, plus a three-pack of V-neck T-shirts for $18.00 for a total of $33.00, and another person purchases two pairs of boxers for $15.00 and a three-pack of crew neck T-shirts for $15.00 for a total of $30.00. Based on the three orders, the average order value for this promotion would be $26 [($15 + $33 + $30) / 3]. This metric can be particularly helpful for evaluating email content or other factors such as timing of an email.

Unsubscribe and Complaint Rates: Number of unsubscriptions or complaints relative to the number of emails sent in a particular campaign. Marketo reports that unsubscription rates are approximately 0.11 to 0.20 percent for typical campaigns and less than 0.10 percent for top-performing campaigns. Unsubscriptions and complaints are inevitable. The key is to try to tie the number of unsubscribers or complainants to other factors. For example, if the company provides a way for people to indicate why they want to be removed from a list, it may be possible to make inferences about the email strategy (e.g., too frequent emails, low relevancy, etc.). Moreover, specific complaints also speak to email strategy as well as the clarity of the emails. Companies should pay careful attention to complaints to make sure that none substantiate a violation of the CAN-SPAM Act. In some instances it may be possible to recapture someone who is about to cancel their subscription by providing options for changing how and when they receive emails.

The Health of an Email List: Growth vs. Churn Rates

One way for an email marketing manager to evaluate the effectiveness of their emails and the health of their email list is to track growth and churn rates. To do so, the manager should generate a report annually (or more frequently) with all of the email addresses, the status (i.e., active, unconfirmed, unsubscribed, bounced, etc.), along with two key dates: the date the email was added and, if applicable, the date when the email was lost.

Let us assume a manager examines the email list semiannually. Then, for the current 6-month period, the manager would measure the growth by counting the number of new email addresses added and comparing it to the growth from the previous period(s) to calculate the percentage change. Similarly, for churn, the manager would count the number of email addresses lost or unsubscribed and compare to the previous period(s) to calculate the percentage change in churn.

If the manager observes decreasing rates of growth, then the manager should investigate what is causing the shift and perhaps implement new strategies for adding addresses to the list (see next chapter). On the other hand, increasing rates of churn over time should raise red flags for a company. Are they offering value with their emails? Are they sending too many? Can the churn rate be associated with any other activities in the marketplace or perhaps a change in IT processes for the company?

Best Practices to Improve Email Performance

1. *Make your identity known and your purpose clear.*

   As discussed, making sure the sender's email address clearly identifies the sender and that the subject line clearly relates to the real purpose of the email is a requirement of the CAN-SPAM Act. However, it also serves another purpose—creating trust. The email recipient is more likely to at least consider opening an email from a sender they trust, as opposed to immediately deleting an email from an unknown, potentially suspicious sender. And if the subject line is consistent with the body of the email, the recipient will also build trust for the sender that whatever the subject line says, the email means. Creating and maintaining trust is a key best practice in email marketing.

2. *Keep it visual—but have a backup plan.*

   As they say, content is king. Because email is such an important tool, and in fact may be the only means a company has for directly reaching customers, it is not uncommon to hire creative agencies that specialize in visual aspects of email design. It is also an opportunity to integrate visual marketing collateral from another channel so that outgoing messages across channels are consistent.

   When deciding whether to use images or not, it is important to remember that some email clients are set to block images by default. Without images loading, most of the body area in the email would appear as missing to the recipient. Moreover, an email that is heavy with images might be flagged as spam or junk email by a spam filter even if the email is legitimate. When designing an email, if the email is heavy in images, each image should include alternate text with key information that will always display. An email designer can ensure that key messages, buttons, and calls to action show up in any email client by using basic HTML and style sheets.

3. *Call to action should stand out and needs to link to an associated landing page.*

   The call to action in an email needs to stand out. It not only clarifies the action that the recipient is expected to take but also establishes a connection with the subject line. Perhaps more importantly, the call to action should link to a special landing page where there is a clear connection with the email. For example, Banana Republic recently sent an email advertising that recipients could take an extra 40 percent off on new women's styles using the code BRNEW (see Figure 4.2). If you visited Banana Republic directly, the promotion would appear as a line item at the top (see Figure 4.3a). However, if you visited Banana Republic via the link in the email, you would be brought to a unique landing page associated with the email where the sale description is larger and clearly identified (see Figure 4.3b).

Figure 4.2 An email promotion from Banana Republic for 40 percent of new styles for women

Figure 4.3a Direct landing page for Banana Republic

Figure 4.3b Landing page for Banana Republic associated with email

4. *Subject lines, Subject lines, Subject lines!*

Perhaps the most critical element is the email subject line. First, the subject line needs to be relevant to the recipient. If it is not, it is unlikely they will open the email. Second, it needs to grab the recipient's attention. Length can play a big role, especially depending on the size of screen that the email is being viewed on. For example, when receiving an email promotion from Hanes.com on a computer screen, the reader may see a preview of the email itself (see Figure 4.4), or they may only see the subject line because of their browser/software setting for accepting graphics or layouts. However, on a mobile device, there is less likely to be a preview screen and hence, for the same email from Hanes.com, only the subject line will appear (see Figure 4.5). Thus, it is critical that the subject line grabs the recipient's attention and creates a desire to open the email. Unfortunately, there is no single correct approach to writing a subject line. What works for one audience may not work for another. Therefore, it is essential to test out variations of subject lines and track over time what type of subject lines are most effective with your customers. We will address how to test email elements in Chapter 7.

5. *Mobile optimization*

As discussed earlier, email marketers need to ensure that their emails are designed not just for laptop or desktop computers but also for mobile devices, with their distinct operating systems, smaller screens, and touch-oriented controls. As touched on in the previous section, marketers need to consider the overall design and message of a mobile email. Messages need to be much shorter, and the buttons and call to action need to be clearer and large enough to tap with a finger on

Figure 4.4 Emails on a computer

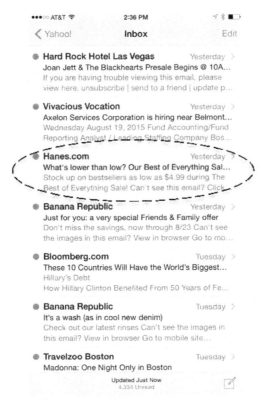

Figure 4.5 Emails on a mobile device

mobile devices. In addition to adjusting the look and feel of the email, marketers also need to think about the landing page that any link in the email will go to. If these web pages are not mobile-friendly, the email may generate click-through traffic, but there will be significant drop-off in other activities.

Exercise: Email Dashboard Spreadsheet

XYZ Company maintains an email list of 100,000 names. Of the emails sent, 99,589 were successfully delivered, 342 were returned because of vacation autoresponse, and the remainder was returned due to invalid or inactive email addresses. There were 12 complaints and a total of 25 recipients who unsubscribed because of frequency of emails that XYZ sends. Of the emails delivered, there were 4,700 unique opens and 1,333 unique click-throughs. In the end, 323 purchases were made with an average order value of $75. The cost of sending the email inclusive of list maintenance and payment for software services was $0.14 per email sent.

Create a spreadsheet connecting all of the metrics discussed above using the formulas provided in this chapter.

1. Calculate delivery rate, overall bounce rate, and soft/hard bounce rates, then evaluate the quality of the list.
2. Calculate open rate, CTR, and CTO rate and evaluate how well the email performed relative to getting the attention of the list.
3. Calculate conversion rate and take into account average order value. How effective was this email overall? Relative to the cost?
4. Based on MarketingSherpa's benchmarks, how would you rate XYZ's email ability—average or exceptional? Explain.

References

Hanna, R.C., P.D. Berger, and L.J. Abendroth. (2005). "Optimizing time limits in retail promotions: An email application," *Journal of the Operational Research Society* 56, no. 1, pp. 15–24.

MailChimp, statistics found at http://mailchimp.com/resources/research/effects-of-list-segmentation-on-email-marketing-stats/ accessed October, 2015.

Marketo. (2013). *The new metrics for email marketing.* Research Report.

Shankaranarayanan, G., E. Adir, and P.D. Berger. (2015). "A decision-analysis approach to optimize marketing information-system configurations under uncertainty," *Journal of Marketing Analytics* 33, no. 1, pp. 14–37.

Swain, S.D., R.C. Hanna, and L.J. Abendroth. (2006). "How time restrictions work: The roles of urgency, anticipated regret, and deal evaluations." In *Advances in Consumer Research,* ed. C. Pechmann and L. Price, vol. 33 (pp. 523–525). San Antonio, TX: Association for Consumer Research.

CHAPTER 5

Consumer Decision Making and the Role of Email

Up to this point, we have discussed the "how" of email marketing by reviewing the fundamentals of email design and common techniques for measuring performance. Let us now move to the questions of "when" and "what" to send. To answer these questions, we must possess a deeper understanding of consumer behavior. Accordingly, in this chapter, we first present a general model of the process consumers go through en route to making decisions about product purchases. Subsequently, we adopt the perspective of marketers who wish to influence or facilitate this process. From this perspective, rather than focusing on the steps consumers go through, we describe a "hierarchy of effects" model that focuses on the stages of a consumer's relationship with a *particular* product or service brand. Throughout, we provide examples of how email can be used to achieve desired marketing outcomes by knowing where consumers stand in their decision-making process as well as the status of their relationship with a particular email marketer's offerings.

Consumer Behavior

Consumer behavior is the process and activities individuals undertake for searching, purchasing, using, and disposing of products and services to satisfy their needs and wants. Some purchase decisions, such as buying a car or camera, may involve lengthy search and evaluation before a purchase can be made. For other purchase decisions, the process may be habitual, such as buying the same brand of orange juice every month, or impulsive, such as adding a pack of mints to your purchase at a checkout counter. Successful marketers can influence consumer behavior if they understand their customers' needs and wants and can reach out to them with the right information at the right time. To do this, we need to learn more about the consumer decision-making process.

Consumer Decision-Making Process

To understand the consumer decision-making process, we draw on the classic "grand models" (e.g., Engel, Kollat, and Blackwell 1968; Howard and Sheth 1969; Nicosia 1966; Olshavsky and Granbois 1979), and present a five-stage conceptualization (see Figure 5.1). The first stage of the consumer decision-making process is *need recognition*. Need recognition can be thought of as either a need to fill a gap or an opportunity to improve one's situation. For example, if a household has used up its last box of Frosted Flakes, then there is a gap that needs to be filled, namely the replacement of a box of cereal. On the other hand, if a person owns an older model of a smartphone and learns of a newer version with improved features that would make the individual's life more productive, then this would be a need based on an opportunity to improve one's situation. Another way to think about need recognition is that it represents an individual's motivation for wanting a particular product. For example, imagine you are planning a trip overseas and you want to focus on taking pictures. You realize that your current Canon digital camera is somewhat dated and you are aware that a newer camera would take better-quality pictures and have some additional features not currently on your camera. If photography is important to you and this trip is special, you might be highly motivated to look into available replacement options.

Once the consumer recognizes a "need," they may engage in *information search*. Initially, this search might be "internal" and consist of examining memories of known or prior solutions (e.g., as represented by awareness of relevant existing products and services). As the individual exhausts what they already know, if needed, they may also conduct an "external" search for information from sources such as friends, coworkers

Figure 5.1 The consumer decision model

(Onyemah, Swain, and Hanna 2010), magazines, social media (Cheong and Park 2015), and online reviews (Weathers, Swain, and Grover 2015). This stage is heavily influenced by which marketing elements capture attention and how the elements are perceived. Continuing our camera example, we may know that Canon has released several newer versions, but we may also know that there are other high-quality, innovative brands we have considered in the past such as Nikon and Sony. However, we may not know exactly what the latest options are, so we go to the Internet and search camera websites, retail stores, blogs, and other media to update our knowledge, thus conducting both internal (memory) and external (e.g., Internet) searches for information.

Once an individual has satisfied their need for information (which will vary from person to person and depending on how involved or high-stakes the decision is), they generally winnow the set of all encountered alternatives down to a smaller set of alternatives that meet some criteria for further consideration. During this *evaluation of alternatives* stage of processing, individuals tend to form strong opinions and attitudes toward the considered set of products or services based on what they have learned and through various methods of comparison. In our camera example, after researching different websites and perhaps speaking to friends, we may narrow the choice set to a newer Canon camera and a new Nikon, eliminating Sony and other brands. At the same time, Canon and Nikon may offer a few different models each that seem acceptable. Evaluating alternatives now involves coming up with a process for comparing our options, such as prioritizing (weighting) attributes or setting minimum or maximum values for attributes, and implementing a procedure for scoring the options. In some cases, consumers may use decision aids such as product configurators or choice-boards (Berger, Hanna, and Swain 2007; Berger et al. 2010).

After evaluating alternatives, consumers are on the precipice of making a *purchase*. In some cases, there may be unexpected events that influence a final purchase such as availability or sales. Once a purchase is made, the individual begins the process of experiencing the product and developing *post purchase attitudes*. In the post purchase stage, consumers are not only influenced by their direct experience with the purchase but also other things that they hear or see. For example, in our camera scenario, let us say we purchased a Canon model and then came across an article indicating the model we chose was nominated for editor's choice on our favorite camera website. In such a case, we are likely to feel even better about our purchase decision. In contrast, if we found out that a camera we did not choose was named editor's choice, we might experience doubts about our decision-making process and our camera. Brand managers are well aware of these possibilities and devote considerable resources helping shape consumers' post purchase attitudes. For example, the brand may reach out and reassure customers about the wisdom of their purchase or provide them with new information about how to get the most out their product or service.

Of course, not all needs require an extensive search or evaluation process. For example, replenishing cereal or buying shampoo may not require significant search and evaluation beyond finding an available source at the lowest price. Additionally, the better the prior experience with a product, the consumer may bypass different stages of this model and move toward purchase.

Marketing Communications Objective: Hierarchy of Effects

As you learn more about marketing and consumer behavior, you may encounter different models marketers use to understand and manage consumer behavior. Many of these models have similar formulations as the consumer decision-making process, except that they are conceptualized from the perspective of customers' dispositions with regard to the marketer's own product or service (McGuire 1978; Rogers 1962; Sheldon 1911). Perhaps the most well-known model of this type is the hierarchy of effects model (see Figure 5.2), which is a representation of how marketing communications may influence the consumer decision-making process over time (e.g., Lavidge and Steiner 1961; Ray et al. 1973). The term hierarchy refers to the notion that earlier "effects" (e.g., awareness) are thought to be generally necessary for achieving subsequent effects (e.g., inform the market). Whereas mass communication marketers can only roughly estimate where the average consumer may be in the hierarchy after a set of communications (e.g., based on ad-tracking results), email marketers may be able to precisely estimate where individual consumers sit in the hierarchy and thus customize subsequent communications.

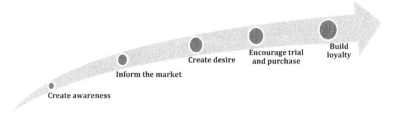

Figure 5.2 The hierarchy of effects model

From a hierarchy of effects perspective, marketing communications must first *create awareness* (or reactivate awareness) in consumers regarding the product or service in question. This same communication might lead to a consumer recognizing an unanticipated need. In our camera example, imagine that we were not thinking about purchasing a new camera for our trip until we came across an advertisement for new features in a Nikon model that allows for easier, higher-quality photos in outdoor settings. In this scenario, Nikon has successfully created awareness for its new model while also helping us recognize a need. Marketers also seek to create marketing communications that *inform the market* of how their products and services work. This may be in the form of digital marketing (e.g., YouTube videos, websites, etc.) or a longer-form advertisement with demonstrations. For example, Nikon may post a video on its website or on YouTube in which the features of its new model are introduced and explained. Once the market is aware of a product or service and has an understanding of what the product or service does or represents, marketers' objectives shift to *create desire*. In general, this means persuading consumers that the product or service is superior in some fashion to its alternatives (e.g., highest quality or best value or best fit). For example, Nikon could air a commercial in which it claims that its new model takes demonstrably better pictures outdoors or that it makes taking good pictures outdoors easier than other brands do. When consumers reach the point of desiring the product or service in question, marketers must design communications, promotions, or events in an effort to *encourage trial and purchase*. That is, the objective is to get the consumer to act on their desire. In the Nikon example, consumers may be offered rebates or a free camera case or they may simply be urged to "act now!" In the final stage of the hierarchy of effects, marketers seek to *build loyalty* among consumers who have tried or purchased the brand. For example, Nikon may engage in brand image advertising to nurture consumers' perception of the brand as unique and favorable and thus self-enhancing. Similarly, consumers can be encouraged to explore idiosyncratic ways to use the product, thereby creating a greater sense of control, personal investment, and intimate knowledge of the product or technology (Kirk, Swain, and Gaskin 2015). Nikon may also take more direct measures, such as offering special amenities or access or discounts to existing customers. In doing so, Nikon is managing consumers' post purchase evaluations and improving its chances of earning future business and avoiding the high costs and significant risks of trying to find new customers and move them through the entire hierarchy of effects (Swain, Berger, and Weinberg 2014).

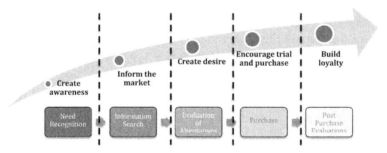

Figure 5.3 *The overlap of the consumer decision process and the hierarchy of effects model*

Using Email Strategically

Marketers typically send emails to consumers in one of two ways: they either push emails directly in a one-to-many format or they automate emails to send to a consumer in response to a triggered action or event. Using a push approach is very similar to sending emails based on the hierarchy of effects. Marketers design an email to achieve a specific objective and send it to their list. However, by using automation, marketers allow emergent consumer behaviors to determine which emails are sent and how they are constructed, thus more directly informing the consumer decision-making model process. Savvy marketers should use both approaches. However, caution is required.

Push Emails

Marketers use push emails, or one-to-many bulk emails, to achieve specific marketing communications objectives. For example, a company launching a new product or updating an existing product may want to generate awareness and thus sends a bulk email to their existing customers (and/or rents a list of email addresses). Despite the bulk nature of the sender, the emails can still be personalized with consumers' names or other information that the company has access to in its customer database or as provided by an email list vendor.

The most common push emails are for sales, lead generation, search engine promotion, and online media. Product or service emails that are consumer-oriented typically announce new products or offer sales promotions (e.g., see Figure 5.4 for a recent Banana Republic push email).

Acquisition emails are focused on either creating new customers by offering a promotion (e.g., retail offer) or free service (e.g., access to white papers) or retaining existing customers (e.g., new product or service announcements, sales, conferences, etc.). These emails will vary in their look and feel depending on the type of business.

Some emails are focused on lead generation and less on immediate conversion. For example, MINI USA (the auto manufacturer) sends out monthly emails to their existing customers announcing updates and changes to MINI as well providing information about events and other activities (see Figure 5.5). Financial planners, lawyers, or consulting firms and other agencies often send out informational emails providing helpful content to try to generate traffic and engagement. For example, financial planners from Ameriprise may send investment tips (see Figure 5.6), while research firms may announce their latest white paper on a relevant topic such as B2B lead generation (see Figure 5.7). While the primary targets are their existing customers, companies sending these types of emails are also counting on their customers to share these emails with friends or other associates.

Figure 5.4 Example of a sales promotion email

Figure 5.5 Example of lead generation and newsletter email

Figure 5.6 Example of services thought leadership email

Figure 5.7 Example of B2B lead generation using a white paper

Online travel agents and other search-engine-oriented companies may send an email announcing their latest deals to encourage their customers to use their search engine or stay top of mind for future searches. For example, Expedia recently sent an email promoting their low-fare alert (see Figure 5.8). Customers who are interested in this opportunity may use Expedia to search for more information. Or, just the idea of taking a trip might spark the use of their search engine to look into other opportunities.

Online media also send regular emails to their lists with content such as stories of the day. By bringing their readers to their website, online media companies generate advertising revenues from the banners that appear and other on-site marketing. For example, WEEI, a popular Boston sports radio station that also maintains their own sports news website, sends out "daily mashup" emails regarding the hot topics of the day (see Figure 5.9).

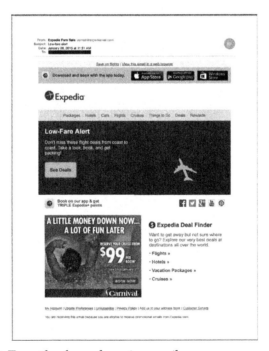

Figure 5.8 Example of search engine email

Figure 5.9 Example of online media emails

Automated Emails

Automated emails, or triggered emails, are emails that are set up to automatically send to the recipient as a result of a specific event. In other words, the marketer creates a custom email template with fill in fields for user data and other customer information. When a condition or a set of conditions is satisfied, the custom email is triggered and automatically sent to the receiver. The key difference between automated and push emails is that there are typically two types of triggers: action triggers and event triggers.

Action triggers are automated emails that are sent as a result of an action that a consumer completed. For example, shopping at a website and abandoning the shopping cart without completing purchase might trigger a reminder email. A customer who has not signed into their account for a long time may receive a welcome-back email. If a person has forgotten their login information, then the automated email that is sent with reset information is also considered a triggered email. However, perhaps the most important triggered email would be a "thank you" email.

We take for granted the value of being acknowledged for a task or deed. Providing a personal email thanking an individual for completing a task, filling out a survey, or some other activity can mean the difference between a casual customer and loyal customer. Other, more functional types of triggered emails include purchase receipts and confirmation emails.

Event triggers are automated emails triggered by an event, such as an upcoming anniversary or scheduled event. For example, if a company wanted to provide a product discount that expires on a recipient's birthday, the automated email could be programmed to trigger a set number of days in advance of the birthday date. A sequence of emails could then be programmed as reminders until the key event passes.

The key benefit of automated emails is that they are in response to consumer behavior. In other words, companies can potentially predict or determine the stage of the consumer decision-making process an individual is in and send a highly relevant email to help influence the process. For example, when an individual fills a shopping basket on a website, they are typically asked to provide an email address early in the process. Thus, when consumers fill a basket but never finish the actual purchase, an automated email is often triggered after a few days to remind the individual about the shopping cart and to perhaps offer an incentive or provide a rationale to complete the purchase. In this case, it is relatively clear the individual was in the purchase stage of their decision process and perhaps only needs a nudge to complete that process.

Tier 1 type commerce companies can apply their behavioral data with outgoing marketing by making recommendations based on past purchases or recent visits. For example, Amazon.com often will send emails making recommendations based on a prior purchase or even make a price change to a product that was browsed (see Figure 5.10). B2B firms also send product-/service-oriented emails.

Onboarding emails are another type of functional email that is critical to maintaining business. When someone joins your email list or signs up for a service or membership, they typically get an onboarding email that welcomes them and provides additional information. These are helpful emails that recipients can file (or not), which also confirm that the sign-up procedure was a success. Opt-in emails are considered onboarding as are initial offers for new membership.

Figure 5.10 Example of recommendation-based email (triggered)

It should be noted that most triggered emails, especially transactional emails, are exempt from the CAN-SPAM Act because they are typically in response to a customers' request or action, and thus are solicited as opposed to unsolicited.

References

Berger, P.D., R.C. Hanna, and S.D. Swain. (2007). "Collaborative Filtering: Advertising Efficiency." In *Media and Advertising Management—New Trends,* ed. *Sabyasachi Chatterjeem,* Hyderabad: ICFAI University Press, pp. 105–111.

Berger, P.D., R.C. Hanna, S.D. Swain, and B.D. Weinberg. (2010). "Configurators/Choiceboards: Uses, Benefits, and Analysis of Data." In *Encyclopedia of E-Business Development and Management in the Global Economy,* ed. Lee, IGI Publishing, pp. 428–435.

Cheong, H. and Park, J.S. (2015). "How do consumers in the Web 2.0 era get information? Social media users' use of and reliance on traditional media," *Journal of Marketing Analytics*, published online, September 7, 2015. doi:10.1057/jma.2015.9

Engel, J.F., D.T. Kollat, and R.D. Blackwell. (1968). *Consumer Behavior*, New York: Holt, Rinehart and Winston.

Howard, J.A. and J.N. Sheth. (1969). *The Theory of Buyer Behavior.* New York: John Wiley and Sons.

Kirk, C., S.D. Swain, and J.E. Gaskin. (2015). "I'm Proud of It: Consumer Technology Appropriation and Psychological Ownership." *Journal of Marketing Theory and Practice* 23, no. 2, 166–184.

Lavidge, R.C. and G.A. Steiner. (1961). "A model for predictive measurements of advertising effectiveness." *Journal of Marketing* 25, pp. 59–62.

McGuire, W.J. (1978). "An information-processing model of advertising effectiveness." In *Behavioral and Management Sciences in Marketing*, eds. H.J. Davis and Al J. Silk. New York: Wiley, pp. 156–180.

Nicosia, F.M. (1966). *Consumer Decision Processes: Marketing and Advertising Implications.* Englewood Cliffs, NJ: Prentice Hall.

Olshavsky, R.W. and D.B. Granbois. (1979). "Consumer decision making—Fact or fiction?" *Journal of Consumer Research* 6, pp. 93–100.

Onyemah, V., S.D. Swain, and R.C. Hanna. (2010). "A Social Learning Perspective on Sales Technology Adoption and Sales Performance: Preliminary Evidence from an Emerging Economy." *Journal of Personal Selling & Sales Management* 30, no. 2, pp.131–142.

Ray, M.L., A.G. Sawyer, M.L. Rothschild, R.M. Heeler, E.C. Strong, and J.B. Reed. (1973). "Marketing communications and the hierarchy of effects." In *New Models for Mass Communication Research*, ed. P. Clarke. Beverly Hills, CA: Sage Publishing.

Rogers, E.M. (1962). *Diffusion of Innovation*, New York: Free Press.

Sheldon, A.F. (1911). *The Art of Selling*, Chicago: The Sheldon School.

Swain, S.D., P.D. Berger, and B.D. Weinberg. (2014). "The Customer Equity Implications of Using Incentives in Acquisition Channels: A Nonprofit Application." *Journal of Marketing Analytics* 2, no. 1, pp. 1–17.

Weathers, D., S.D. Swain, and V. Grover. (2015). "Can Online Product Reviews be More Helpful? Examining Characteristics of Information Content by Product Type," *Decision Support Systems* 79 (November), pp. 12–23.

CHAPTER 6

Making a List That Is Worth Its Weight in Gold

A company's email list is a vital organizational asset. Assuming the list was built organically and not purchased, most, if not all, of the names on the list have a specific connection with the company. That connection can be nourished and strengthened with appropriate email communications. Also, the more that is known about customers (e.g., first contact, method of first contact, demographics, buying history, etc.), the greater the likelihood a company can identify the right and most relevant opportunities to reach out with highly targeted and personal communications. The challenge is building this list the right way and keeping track of the right information. In this chapter, we will discuss the thought process for building an email list and methods to increase sign-ups. We will also discuss issues around the process of signing-up, such as amount of personal information to collect and whether to use a single- or double-opt-in process.

Building a List, Checking It Twice. . .

Building an email list from the ground up, requires mapping out all of the potential points of contact or **sources of contact** with existing and potential customers. We have grouped the most common sources of contact into four categories (see Figure 6.1): personal sources, Internet sources, referral sources, and outside engagement sources. Personal sources include any opportunity to connect directly with people as part of doing business. For example, when an individual makes a purchase in a store and provides an email address while checking out. Another direct opportunity is when a company fields a phone call from a customer who might be requesting information or looking for customer

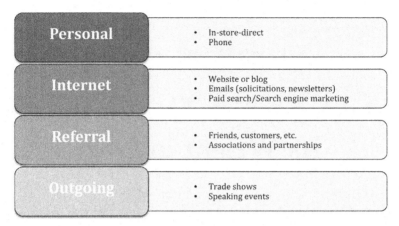

Figure 6.1 Sources of contact for building email lists

service. Essentially, any everyday business task that involves directly interacting with a customer is an opportunity to add to your list. Internet sources include any interaction a customer has with a company in the digital world. For example, if a person visits a company's website or a related blog. There should be an automated process or exchange that allows the company to solicit the individual's email address. Even creating an opportunity to provide an email address within another email is important. For example, a customer who receives an email newsletter might forward that email to a friend who is not on the list. Having a sign-up action area that brings this new potential customer to a sign-up landing page increases the likelihood of adding that person to the list.

A third source is referrals. Some companies have a formal referral program, whereas others may have partnerships with other companies or organizations. For example, a sporting goods store may have a special relationship with a local sporting training school. In the process of signing-up for the school program, a person could opt-in to receiving an email from the sporting goods store to buy the appropriate equipment or clothing. A contact that is made based on an existing relationship is a key opportunity to reach a warm audience. The fourth source is through engagement opportunities such as trade shows, speaking engagements, or other appearances in a new environment. Either by collecting names at a booth or by working with conference organizers to collect names of those who attended a keynote speech, collecting emails from individuals interested in a related topic or where your company is the point of discussion is another key opportunity to add to an email list.

It Is Less about Privacy and More about Value

Some individuals may be concerned about sharing their email address because of privacy concerns or fear that they will be overwhelmed with solicitations. However, most of these concerns can be overcome if the requestor is offering something of value. For example, when making a purchase in a store, a cashier may ask a customer for their email address as part of the checkout process. This creates an awkward moment. While consumers understand in general terms how the marketplace and its social actors work (John 1999; Vohs, Baumeister, and Chin 2007; Wright 2002; Wright, Friestad, and Boush 2005), they also remain wary of the motivations marketers have for specific behaviors (Darke and Ritchie 2007; Kramer 1999; Main, Dahl, and Darke 2007). Many customers may contemplate what the store wants with their email address and what the potential outcomes of sharing their address will be. From the cashier's perspective, requesting the email address is just a matter of store policy. Now let us revisit this same situation but provide an incentive.

What if upon checking out the cashier asked the customer if they would prefer an electronic receipt instead of a paper receipt? The cashier could also tell the customer, if they are not already aware, that the advantage (i.e., value) of the e-receipt is they are less likely to lose it and it will make returning any items purchased simpler. Now, instead of contemplating what the company will be doing with their email, the customer is considering the benefit (i.e., value) of this e-receipt. Thus, the preconditions for a win–win exchange have been established: the store provides a service in the way of an electronic receipt in exchange for access to an individual's email address. Research has shown that people tend to self-disclose more about themselves the more they like the person they are talking to or if the other person self-discloses first (Collins and Miller 1994). So it should be no surprise that providing an incentive or explaining how sharing an email address can facilitate greater service would enhance the likelihood of self-disclosure.

There are many ways companies can offer value in exchange for an individual's email (see Figure 6.2). For example, a retailer may connect the exchange of an email address with joining a loyalty program. The Container Store has the POP! Star loyalty program where customers provide their email address and in exchange they are enrolled in a program that provides many of the standard loyalty perks (see Figure 6.3). Additionally, customers automatically receive e-receipts while also maintaining a record of the purchase receipt, thus eliminating the need for the customer to even worry about finding a receipt should they need to return or exchange an item.

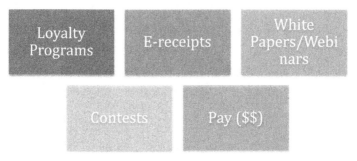

Figure 6.2 Examples of marketing inventory that a company can exchange for an email address

Figure 6.3 Container store's POP! Loyalty program

Running a contest or a giveaway not only provides value to the customer but it also provides an opportunity to increase engagement with the company if the event is tied in with social media. Service firms can provide a free e-book or whitepaper in exchange for an email and contact information.

In some cases, it may be simpler just to pay money directly for email addresses. For example, when you visit BananaRepublic.com, you are immediately greeted with an opportunity to provide your email for a 25% discount (see Figure 6.4). A company could take a more direct approach and literally offer $1 to $5 for an email address. For example, in a recent visit to the local CVS Pharmacy store, the cashier asked whether one of the authors would be willing to provide their email address in exchange for $3.00 in-store credit. It is now up to CVS to make sure that subsequent contacts are valuable or this could easily be $3.00 wasted. Alternatively, a company can rent a list of addresses from a credit card company or similar organizations. The upside to renting a list is the quick turnaround. The downside is that the people on the list may have no real connection to the sender and may automatically delete or potentially complain about receiving an email that they do not recall signing up for.

Figure 6.4 Banana Republic offer of discount in exchange for email address

In sum, companies should continually assess the cost of acquiring an email address through the different contact opportunities and also assess what short- and long-term value is returned to the company by those email addresses. For example, imagine a research and consulting firm that is trying to add new email addresses to their existing database. Let us assume they have recently offered the following in exchange for an email address: a white paper with a cost of $7,000 to create, a webinar with a cost of $5,000 to run, and a contest with a $2,500 prize. If each of the activities led to acquiring 4,000, 1,000, and 10,000 unique emails, respectively, the least costly method for acquiring email addresses is running a contest (see Table 6.1). However, reading a white paper or participating in a webinar is likely to provide a stronger connection with the names on that list and they may have a better understanding of the quality of services provided by the focal company. Hence, they may be more likely to purchase a future report or service knowing the quality and level of expertise that was displayed in the sample white paper or webinar. To consider the impact of these factors, let us assume that the revenue derived from these new addresses through subsequent email campaigns over the next 12 months is $200,000 for the emails generated by the white paper offer, $100,000 from the webinar emails, and $50,000 from the contest emails. Thus, on a revenue-per-email basis, offering the white paper in exchange for an email has better long-term value of the three tactics. The contest which had the lowest cost per email acquired, has the least long-term return of the three. While the webinar is in the middle of the three approaches, it is interesting to note in this case it has the best return per email sent of the three tactics. Companies should regularly conduct these types of analyses to confirm that they are optimizing their approach to acquiring email addresses.

Table 6.1 An example of cost and revenue from email-generating activities

Method	Cost	Unique emails acquired	Cost per email	Revenue over the next 12 months from new list	Revenue per email
White Paper	$7,000	4,000	$1.75	$200,000	$50
Webinar	$5,000	1,000	$5.00	$100,000	$100
Contest	$2,500	10,000	$0.25	$50,000	$5

Not Just Who, but Why. . .

In addition to the actual email address and the method by which it was acquired, it is helpful to track other information regarding the acquisition context. For example, if an email address is collected in the store, is it associated with a purchase or a request for information? If it was a purchase, what was the value of the purchase? Was this purchase the individual's first purchase at the store or have they previously purchased?

Other types of information that can be collected or associated with an email include demographic data such as zip code, gender, and age for B2C-oriented products and services or company size, position, and industry for B2B-oriented products and services. Ideally, one would establish the ability to continually track customer behavior and update an email list regularly. However, not all companies have the data infrastructure to capture such details. We will discuss some of the advantages of having more data than less in Chapter 10.

Permission FIRST, Not Forgiveness Later

As mentioned in Chapter 2, the CAN-SPAM Act of 2003 does not require a commercial emailer to obtain permission to send an email to an individual. However, most email-marketing experts will tell you that sending an email without prior permission is a poor choice. In fact, professional emails services, such as MailChimp and Constant Contact, have specific rules against emailing without permission. The best course of action is to obtain permission to send an email before sending that email. If you are not sure you have it, assume you do not. Moreover, it helps to keep a record of how the email address is acquired (e.g., in store, website, exchange for whitepaper, etc.) in case the company needs to prove that they are in compliance.

Let us be clear about permission to send an email. By asking for permission, you are asking an individual to "opt-in" to receiving an email or other communication. The opposite, opt-out, would be asking the individual if they would like to decline receiving emails. The distinction between these two actions has strategic implications. In 2011, Barnes & Noble Bookstores (B&N) completed the purchase of competitor, Borders Bookstores. As part of the purchase, B&N also acquired Border's email list from their loyalty program. Rather than ask if Border's customers would like to remain with B&N, hence opt-in to the new program, B&N sent an email giving Border's customers the chance to opt-out as long as they did so by a specific date. This action angered many of the Border's customers and generated negative press for B&N. Thus it is critical when obtaining an email address that the company makes clear that they are also asking for permission to communicate with the individual. If an email list is acquired, as in the example of B&N, then it is up to the company to renew this relationship by asking again if the individuals want to opt-in to the new company.

The Opt-In Process and List Maintenance

As described earlier in the chapter, when requesting someone's email, there is also an opportunity to ask for additional information. For example, in a retail store, the cashier may ask for an email address and the individual's zip code. If the request is coming online, then the individual may be required to fill in a pop-up form that asks additional questions about them. Alternatively, additional information can be built up over time. For example, when an individual email is collected verbally in a store, this could trigger a welcome email confirming the opt-in and requesting more information.

One key to increasing likelihood of opt-in (beyond offering incentives and explaining the value of opting-in) is to keep the initial process as simple and as quick as possible. To do this, a company needs to evaluate how much (or really, how little) information they need up front from an individual to communicate with them effectively. Although more information is generally better than less information, it is not wise to jeopardize the success of opt-ins by asking for too much. It is important to take a long-term view and consider the company's abilities and opportunities to augment customer data over time.

For example, many national retailers send frequent emails to their customer list without targeting based on a specific gender or age or other demographic or behavioral variable. In such cases where there is no immediate plan for targeted emails, the best opt-in design is to use the simplest process possible—gather only the email address (e.g., see Banana Republic's opt-in tactic in Figure 6.4). To add more information about an individual, they could simply be invited to join a loyalty program where there is an added benefit to providing additional information.

Another important consideration is assuring that an email address acquired is valid. Most opt-in processes require an individual to type their email address in two different fields to assure that they type it accurately. However, this does not assure that the email address is valid. It just assures that the person can replicate their provision (or that they know how to use copy/paste commands). Instead, it is recommended that, where possible, companies should use a double-opt-in approach. A double-opt-in process means that an individual is not officially signed up (and hence receives anything in exchange) until the email address has been confirmed. To do this, upon the initial sign-up, a confirmation email is triggered and sent to the email address provided. In the confirmation email, the recipient will be asked to validate their sign-up by clicking a provided hyperlink, hence opting-in a second time. Alternatively, a company may also pay for a third-party verification tool to assure that the email address entered is legitimate. Either of these procedures provides assurance that the email address entered is valid and reduces the likelihood of imposters' accidental opt-ins due to typographical errors by the user (e.g., johnsmith@gmail.con).

The Nuts and Bolts of Segmentation and Targeting

So why segment and target? Customers are diverse in their needs, so to satisfy everyone with one offer or message can be difficult. Trying to please everyone or "the average consumer" can leave the organization vulnerable to more focused competitors at every differentiable point in the market. To recount a popular example in marketing strategy courses: if half of the people prefer hot tea and the other half prefer cold tea, then marketers who fail to segment will conclude that the "average" consumer prefers lukewarm tea. This, of course, is a recipe for dramatic failure since *no one* in the market prefers lukewarm tea. A further benefit of segmentation is greater efficiency, since less effort is wasted by saying the wrong things to the wrong people or by engaging with individuals who are not even in the target market. The advantages of segmentation are clear, as evidenced by a 2012 study by BtoB Magazine stating that 84% of B2B marketers use segment targeting in their email campaigns (Hosford 2012).

Ultimately, segmentations are judged on their ability to enhance outcomes on key metrics. Since there are multiple metrics that matter, there may be multiple valid segmentations. At the customer level, such metrics may include historical or current valuations such as revenue, profit, or cash flow. However, many companies also care about indicators of potential value, including lifetime value, up-sell/cross-sell potential, or share of wallet. At the brand level, common metrics include brand image/equity, momentum, or share of loyal customers in the market.

List segmentation depends on having data on your customers as well as the actual existence or nonexistence of underlying segments along the dimensions spanned by the data. Each data type, or variable, becomes something you can use to search for meaningful differences (with respect to focal metrics) among customers. For example, if you have tracked when a customer first joined the email list, this variable can be used to distinguish between long- and short-tenure customers. This difference may matter, not because of tenure per se, but because of the different nature of the customer–company relationship and the attending implications for managing the relationship. To this point, segmentations must be dynamic. Consumers' situations, requirements, and expectations evolve over time and marketers must continually examine the mix of individual statuses in a market of interest. Other variables that frequently serve as segmentation bases include zip code, profession, gender, average order size, recency of last purchase, and frequency of purchases in a calendar year. Tier-1 commerce companies (see Chapter 1) use historical behavioral data for predictive modeling and can segment based on an expected action (e.g., purchase timing).

Despite the potential advantages of segmentation, it relies on differences that emerge along observable dimensions, and there is no guarantee that these dimensions have anything to do with differences in consumers' requirements. For example, we may segment customers based on differentiated lifestyle characteristics only to learn (the hard way) that lifestyle is not important in terms of how consumers relate to the product category. Alternatively, even when we use "good" segmentation bases, it still may turn out that it is infeasible to properly serve our preferred target segments given our sales and media channel configurations. Additionally, the way that segments react to marketing levers (elasticities) may differ such that the profitability of designing and delivering multiple effective email communications is lower than that of simply using a nonsegmented approach. Thus, segmentation is a moving target.

After segmenting the email list, the next step is to determine how to approach one or more segments with a highly targeted message or offer.

Measuring the Impact of Blast Emails vs. Targeted Emails

As discussed, companies can segment their list and send highly targeted offers to subgroups within their email list. Interestingly, over 80% of email marketers send the same content to all subscribers (Experian 2014). Not only does this increase the likelihood an individual receives an email that is less relevant but it also potentially leaves money on the table as marketers may be sending the wrong type of message to many of their customers.

Artbeads.com, an online jewelry supply shop, increased their conversion rate by 208% by using a targeted email instead of blasting the same email to all of their customers (Moran 2012). Artbeads.com used a service provided by Windsor Circle (a vendor of marketing automation software) to evaluate the buying behavior of their customer list. Using this information, they sent a targeted end-of-season promotional email to only 2% of their total list, which generated a conversion rate four times larger than when they sent it to their entire list. By not sending the same email to the entire list, they reduced the risk of exhausting all of their customers with nonrelevant emails and instead sent a subgroup of names offers that differed in type or timing. MailChimp, an email service provider, has found that list segmentation and targeting increases unique open rates by approximately 12% and clicks by 53% compared to nonsegmented email blasts. Acxiom, a marketing technology and services company compared the performance results of similar clients using blast emails versus targeted emails. While the cost per email using a targeted approach was $0.14 per email compared to $0.04 per email due to the additional cost of tracking and integrating customer data, the revenue generated by targeted emails was 3.5 times greater than that generated by the blast emails.

Managing Lists with Software and Third-Party Vendors

Once you have got the list assembled, the next step is to find a way to efficiently send out and report on your email. For professional marketing, you will want to avoid an approach that involves simply putting all of the addresses in the bcc line in Outlook as discussed in Chapter 3. This approach is fraught with danger.

Instead, you will want to select an email-marketing technology platform. There are two categories of platforms—those oriented for small businesses and those oriented for enterprise applications. Both will handle the creation of email using a template or custom email, testing and previewing, basic list management, and reporting on opens, clicks, and link activity. Small business applications include web-based platforms like Constant Contact, MailChimp, Bronto, and Vertical Response. These are suitable for most single person to midsized businesses that are working from a single, static list.

The enterprise applications will add advanced features to help with segmentation, list management, reporting, and working with larger data sets.

- List management can be linked to CRM software, and lists can be created on-the-fly using segmentation rules.
- Dynamic publishing in the email allows portions of the email content to be driven by segmentation attributes.
- Advanced reporting features and visualization

Example 1: Understanding Segments—Hotel Business

One major hotel firm that we worked with developed an email list with over 200 attributes for each of its customers. These attributes included items such as:

- Last visit
- Number of nights stayed
- Loyalty program status
- Business versus leisure traveler
- Last minute purchaser

The hotel chain used these attributes to generate segments. They had established segments—such as "road warriors"—that they would think about developing offers for in every email. However, using the rich attribute data, the hotel never sent just one "road warrior" email. They would use the data to fill in the offers based on other behaviors. For example, a road warrior who had stayed with them in the last 30 days and was a member of the loyalty program would get a different offer than a road warrior who had not stayed recently. This type of microsegmentation allowed for the fine-tuning of offers that would produce over one million dollars in sales per email.

Example 2: Branching Out from Your Segments

Although segmentations are essential to creating targeted emails, it is important to not restrict your segments too tightly. In one instance, we learned of a national retailer who was preparing an email for their "new mothers" segment. This was a well-defined segment in their database based on purchase transaction history of diapers, toys, car seat, and other newborn sundries. The email was a product-driven offer that was aimed at driving people to purchase more baby items online.

In the production process, the email was inadvertently sent to the entire email list of the retailer. This is a career-ending type of mistake in some companies. But, in this case, the email was a smashing success. Although the email was not targeted (by any definition), it outperformed previous "new mothers" emails, produced no angry customers, and actually expanded the list of "new mothers."

More recently, another client in the high-end travel and tour industry vastly improved the impact of their email program by expanding the offers in their emails. This company had a very loyal base of customers who took multiple international trips with them each year. Their email open rates are three to four times the industry benchmarks. However, they were sending emails only about tours that customers had explicitly expressed interest in. By adjusting the content of their emails to branch out and offer related tours in addition to the primary tour, the company was able to increase the business generated from these emails.

Exercise: Ice Skate Shop

Imagine a small business such as a local ice skate shop that sells, rents, repairs, and sharpens ice skates. In addition to the retail store, the business also has a web page that it uses to post information about the store and its products, but is not a commerce site or a Facebook page. The business has a phone and an email address for the store. They also work with a local ice-skating school that teaches both kids and adults how to skate.

Questions:

1. How many sources of contact with a potential customer does this small business have? What types of source are these?

2. What should this small business offer in exchange for a customer's email address?

3. What type of information about the customer should the store try to maintain? How would you recommend they use that information?

4. If one type of customers are the parents of children learning to skate and these customers typically purchase a new pair of skates (~$50) every year for around 5 years, what should the store be willing to spend to acquire the email addresses of these customers?

References

Collins, N.L. and M.L. Carol. (1994). "Self-disclosure and liking: A meta-analytic review." *Psychological Bulletin* 116, no. 3, pp. 457–475.

Darke, P.R. and R.J.B. Ritchie. (2007). "The defensive consumer: Advertising deception, defensive processing, and trust." *Journal of Marketing Research* 44, no. February, pp. 114–127.

Experian. (2014). "Q3 2014 Email Benchmark Report." *Quarterly Email Benchmark Reports*, Experian Marketing Services.

Hosford, C. (2012). "BtoB study: Marketers using digital channels to boost brands." *BtoB Magazine* 97, no. 3, p. 3.

John, D.R. (1999). "Consumer socialization of children: A retrospective look at twenty-five years of research." *Journal of Consumer Research* 26, no. 3, pp. 183–213.

Kramer, R.M. (1999). "Trust and distrust in organizations: Emerging perspectives, enduring questions." *Annual Review of Psychology* 50, pp. 569–598.

Main, K., D. Dahl, and P. Darke. (2007). "Deliberative and automatic bases of suspicion: Empirical evidence of the sinister attribution error." *Journal of Consumer Psychology* 17, no. 1, pp. 59–69.

Moran, G. (2012). "How customer data can help build better marketing campaigns," Entrepreneur.com, August 13, 2012 (http://www.entrepreneur.com/article/223788 accessed May, 2015).

Vohs, K.D., R.F. Baumeister, and J. Chin. (2007). "Feeling duped: Emotional, motivational, and cognitive aspects of being exploited by others." *Review of General Psychology* 11, no. 2, pp. 127–141.

Wright, P. (2002). "Marketplace metacognition and social intelligence." *Journal of Consumer Research* 28, no. March, pp. 677–682.

Wright, P., M. Friestad, and D.M. Boush. (2005). "The development of marketplace persuasion knowledge in children, adolescents, and young adults." *Journal of Public Policy & Marketing* 24, no. 2, pp. 222–233.

CHAPTER 7

Optimizing Emails and A/B Testing

When is the right time to send an email? Is this the best subject line? Should I use the green background or the blue background? The answer to these questions and others is often "it depends." That is not the answer most people want to hear but it is the smart answer when considering the likely heterogeneous and complexly configured characteristics of your audience in relation to the goal of the email. For example, according to the *2013 Email Marketing Benchmark Report* by MarketingSherpa (2013), retail and B2C ecommerce companies report greater effectiveness for emails sent on Mondays and Tuesdays than on any other days, while Videogame and Software companies are better off sending on Tuesdays and Thursdays. How do they know? Testing. What is the shelf life of these answers? Probably fairly short. Do these answers apply to individual companies? Maybe . . . maybe not. How can we find out? Programmatic testing.

In email marketing, the most common type of testing is called an A/B test. As the name suggests, the basic structure of an A/B test involves sending out "Version A" to one subsample of a list and "Version B" to a different subsample. Ideally, the versions differ in terms of a single element. For example, one subgroup may see an interrogative style subject line ("Do you want a wardrobe as unique as you are?"), while a second subgroup sees a command style subject line ("Get a wardrobe as unique as you are"). The email marketer then compares the two versions in terms of metrics of interest (e.g., open rates, click-to-open, or conversion). If one subject line proves more effective in the test, it is used in emails sent to the remainder of the relevant portion of the email list.

A/B testing is a seemingly simple concept. Perhaps, this is why we see so many companies doing it in ways that seem procedurally correct yet are actually fatally flawed. In our experience, the root of this widespread (yet largely undiagnosed) problem is a lack of understanding of the fundamentals of experimentation. We are not speaking colloquially here. When we say "experimentation" we mean it in the scientific and statistical sense, not in the "I'm in college and want to try new things" sense. In this chapter, we will discuss the fundamentals of marketing experiments and how this relates to proper A/B testing. We will also provide an example of an A/B test that was mishandled to illustrate both the power and pitfalls of A/B testing in the wild.

Test What?

MarketingSherpa surveyed 1,095 marketers and found that 81% performed some form of testing or optimization of their commercial emails. Of these, 59% used data from past campaigns while 47% used active testing. According to MarketingSherpa, of those marketers who test email with some form of A/B testing, the three most commonly tested elements were subject lines (86%), calls-to-action (62%), and messages (58%). According to MailJet, an email service provider, U.S. and German companies are more likely to test subject lines in emails than companies from anywhere else around the world (see Figure 7.1).

	Global Average	USA	France	Germany
Subject lines	39%	44%	27%	44%
Email content areas	37%	37%	30%	45%
Sent dates/times	36%	33%	38%	37%
Sender address	32%	28%	36%	35%
Images	30%	19%	36%	36%
Offers and promotions	28%	31%	25%	30%
Preheaders	23%	21%	30%	18%

Figure 7.1 Comparison of types of AB tests conducted by companies from around the world

Source: http://marketingland.com/report-u-s-companies-send-emails-global-average-1-47-million-sent-per-month-114180

Example: Brooks Brothers—When to Schedule Emails?

Jason is up around 6:30 each morning, dressed and in the kitchen by 7:15 when he grabs his phone off the charger for his first look at his email. Recently, he noticed that almost every morning, sitting at the top of his inbox was an email from Brooks Brothers. In looking at his email history, every other email he received from Brooks Brothers came within 5 minutes of 7:15 am: 7:08, 7:08, 7:09, 7:11, 7:10. Using open-rate analysis, Brooks Brothers figured out what time Jason starts his day and scheduled their messages to arrive when he first picks up his phone. This scheduling means their email is almost always the first email he sees every day. They get him when he is still waking up and vulnerable. Has he bought anything? Nope. But he does notice these messages first thing in the morning, more so than he does with other emails he gets later in the day when he scans down the list of unread emails and just swipes and delete everything unrelated to actual business.

A/B Testing: Think of It as Conducting an Experiment

What is the first thing you think of when you hear the word "experiment"? For some, this might conjure up some ideas of lab rat experimentation or chemistry. For others, it might bring back memories of trying something for the first time. For marketing, experimentation is common practice to test the effectiveness of ad copy and layout, the impact of price changes, responsiveness to product ideas, taste tests, and much more—essentially, anything related to the 4P's (i.e., product, price, place, and promotion). The key to all experiments is that we are looking to see how one object or variable affects a change in another object or variable. This is different than a correlation where we might see that one variable is high and the other is low. With an experiment, we want to see if there is an observable change in one variable due to the other variable. Although this may sound easy, the challenge is making sure to isolate the cause and effect from any other variable that exists in the environment.

For example, companies such as Proctor & Gamble (P&G) create shopping labs where they build their own store where they can control the look of the store, placement of items on a shelf, and the prices of competing products. If P&G is launching a new product and wants to test how consumers will interact with it based on shelf placement, they would invite research subjects to shop in the "lab" and observe and record the interactions and decisions made by these shoppers. In a real store, P&G would have less control over the shelf position without considerable cost and would not be able to control for a random promotion run by a competitor.

Thus, there are three necessary conditions for any experiment to assure that claims about a causal relationship between two variables are (internally) valid:

1. *Temporal ordering*—The cause (i.e., the independent variable) should precede the effect (i.e., the dependent variable) in time. For example, a new email graphic can not be said to impact a click-through rate if it is introduced after the click-through data was collected. While this may seem obvious in a simple example, failure to ensure temporal ordering is a common mistake in the real world where data have complex structures and are often recorded, analyzed, and interpreted by distinct persons at distinct time points.
2. *Concomitant variation*—Changes in the independent variable should be accompanied by observable changes in the dependent variable. This also means that when the independent variable is not changing, no changes should be observed in the dependent variable.
3. *Control of other factors*—Researchers must rule out competing explanations for a proposed causal relationship. For example, a marketer may attribute increased sales in a city to a newly introduced strategy when in fact the increase is more directly attributable a broader industry trend or increases in local disposable income.

Why A/B Testing Can Go Horribly Wrong and You Will Not Even Know It?

Many marketers complain that their A/B testing does not lead to actionable results. Perhaps, this is why MarketingSherpa has found that less than half of their survey respondents conduct A/B tests at all. While it is possible that the two things being compared render no difference in the outcome variable, it is also possible that the experiment has been confounded, or muddied, by some other event or action. There are several issues that can come up in the design of the A/B test and in the process of running the A/B test that should be addressed in advance of the test, or taken into consideration while evaluating the results.

Design Issues

Interactive testing effect—When some other recent interaction with the list member impacts the response to the focal email (e.g., they were sent a related email the day before).

Selection bias—The recipients who receive version A should be nearly identical in nature to those who receive version B. In other words, you do not want recipients who receive version A to be significantly different in profile from those who receive version B (Lo and Pachamanova 2015). For example, if you were to test the subject line for a promotional email and it turns out that the group who sees version A happens to contain a significantly larger percentage of frequent buyers than those who see version B then the effect of version A of the subject line will be overestimated. The best way to avoid this problem is to make sure that names are drawn at random from the entire list to fill each group. Randomization can be more challenging in other contexts. For example, A/B testing on emails that are sent out based on behavioral triggers need to be randomized with respect to time since customers are self-selecting into the overall sample by virtue of choosing to engage in the behavior(s) of interest.

Focusing on more than one variable at a time—There is a tendency to want to test everything at once. However, this can make it difficult to attribute changes in the outcome variable to any one specific independent variable. An A/B test is specifically about manipulating one variable at a time. Going beyond one variable moves into the realm of multivariate testing, which can be done, but requires a more sophisticated process and analysis, which is beyond the scope of this book.

Process Issues

History—Specific events that are external to the experiment but occur at the same time as the experiment. For example, a competitive offer that is run at the same time as your test.

Maturation—The changes in the email recipients themselves that occur with the passage of time. This is less of an issue when the experiment is a short-term (i.e., only a few days versus a month or longer).

Mortality—Differential dropouts prior to measured outcome.

Example: Cloud Service Company

A cloud service firm (henceforth referred to as Sky)[1] was running a conference on cloud services with several keynote speakers from prominent retail and service firms. An email communication related to the conference was to be sent to their list of digital marketing professionals and IT specialists. Each email contained information about the keynote speakers as well as details about the conference and a call-to-action to click-through for more information and to sign up. There were five keynote speakers planned, including four digital marketing professionals and one IT specialist, collectively representing retail, consumer services, and consumer goods sectors.

The IT manager for Sky who was handling the email campaign wanted to test two different subject lines:

A: Cloud Digital Marketing Event
B: Learn from XYZ Hotel and M&N Info Services[2] at this Cloud Marketing Event

The manager assembled a list of 30,000 emails from Sky's customer database. The list consisted of two types of professionals, digital marketing managers and IT specialists. The manager split the list into two groups of 15,000 and sent the conference email with subject line A to group A and an identical email with subject line B to group B. After a period of time, the manager collected the data and examined the open rates and click-through rates for the two subject lines (see Table 7.1).

---

[1] The cloud service firm's real name has been disguised. The data used is based on a real email campaign that was tested. However, some details have been modified or adjusted to protect the identity of the firm.

[2] These were two well-known, well-established companies, but we have disguised the names for privacy purposes.

Table 7.1 Open rate and click-through rate for AB test of email

	Group A: Short subject line	Group B: Long subject line
Number sent to customer list	15,000	15,000
Number of emails opened by list	750	900
Open rate	5.0%	6.0%
Clicks	81	26
Click-through to open rate	10.8%	2.9%

The manager noted that group B with the more detailed subject line performed slightly better on open rates than group A. However, group A had higher click-through to open rates. Somewhat confused by these results, the manager quickly concluded that shorter subject lines have better click-through to open rates, but having a more detailed subject line improved open rates. The manager gave less weight to open rates in this case because the difference was only 1% compared to the larger difference in click-through to open rates. Because the results were mixed, the manager used his gut intuition on subsequent email blasts for this campaign and chose to use the shorter subject line.

There are at least two major issues with this A/B test that should raise red flags. First, we need to know how groups A and B were formed. Was the list presorted in some fashion? What algorithm was used to assign individuals to a group? We can see that the group sizes were equal, but we do not know how they came to be that way. Second, we know that the customer list involved two meaningfully different types of professionals (digital marketing managers versus IT specialists). It is highly plausible that the content of the email was differentially relevant to these customer types. In particular, we observed that the keynote speaker list is predominantly digital marketers; thus the event may have less appeal to IT professionals. Because we are unsure how the group assignments were done, we are now also concerned about whether the two types of speakers are equally represented in the two groups. Otherwise, the results may be more strongly determined by how the groups were formed rather than how the subject lines impact customer responses.

Although we did not encounter this A/B test until the email marketing campaign was over, the Sky manager wondered if there was something he could learn from the experience and provided us with a further breakdown of the data (see Table 7.2). Confirming our concerns, the two groups did not have the same number of customer types in each group. Although this is not problematic per se, it belies the bigger issues. The manager had originally cut the list into two groups without any consideration for the order of the names in the list. In doing so, he violated a major requirement in any experiment that participants be randomly assigned to treatments (in this case, group A or group B). In looking at Table 7.2, we can see that group A has an even split of digital marketers and IT professionals, which is a good sign. It does not imply random assignment (indeed at this point we know the assignment was not randomized), but it is consistent with what we would expect to see under random assignment. However, group B consists of almost all IT professionals. This is alarming and clearly reflects the fact that random assignment was not present in the test.

Breaking the open rates down by type of professional, a very different story from the original begins to emerge. For the shorter subject line, IT professionals had a higher open rate than did digital marketers. However, for the more detailed subject line, digital marketers had a much higher open rate compared to IT professionals. The click-to-open rate is even more telling in this breakdown. Across the board, the click-to-open rate was much higher for digital marketing professionals in both groups, likely because the number of keynote speakers related to their field was higher. However, we cannot draw any strong conclusions since the effect of subject line length on customer responses was never isolated from effect of preexisting, meaningful differences between customers (digital marketers versus IT professionals).

If Sky were to do this again, we would recommend that they do two things. First, confirm that the email they want to send is relevant to their entire list. If the one email does not have the same relevancy to the list, then this is something that should be addressed as a separate test, namely the relevancy of the content. Second, if the list has identifying variables such as profession or some other distinction, then subdivide the list by this variable and make sure each version of the email is sent in equal amounts to these subgroups (e.g., marketers versus IT specialists).

Table 7.2 *Open rate and click-through rate for AB test of email by customer type*

	Group A: Short subject line		Group B: Long subject line	
	Digital marketing profes-sionals	IT profes-sionals	Digital marketing profes-sionals	IT profes-sionals
List breakdown	50%	50%	5%	95%
N	7,500	7,500	750	14,250
Number opened	300	450	60	840
Open rate among group	4.0%	6.0%	8%	6%
Open rate among all	40%	60%	7%	93%
Clicks	69	12	21	5
Click-through to open rate among group	23.0%	2.7%	35.0%	0.6%
Click-through to open rate among all	9.2%	1.6%	2.3%	0.6%

Exercise: Design Your Own AB Test

Imagine you were in charge of promoting a new book (the choice of genre is up to you). You need to send an email out to your list of 100,000 prospects who have purchased at least one book in this genre in the last 6 months and 100,000 prospects who have not purchased in this genre in the last 6 months but have purchased similar books in the past.

1. Would you send the same email to both types of customers? Explain.
2. Assume you are targeting prospects who have made a recent purchase. Sketch out the following details: What would you use for a subject line? What would you include in the body of the email? What would be your call to action?
3. Now do the same for those who have not purchased recently. How similar are the emails? Where, if at all, are they different?
4. Evaluate your email. Who is the target audience? Is it both types of customers?
5. Imagine your manager wants you to conduct an A/B test on the email for recent customers. He is concerned that people will not

open the email and then click-through. What should you test first? Do you need more than one test?

6. Based on the previous question, design your A/B test(s). Assuming you need at least 10,000 people for one test, how would you draw your sample from your list of 200,000 total names? When would you send the emails? What will you vary in your two emails? Explain.

References

Lo, V.S.Y. and D.A. Pachamanova. (2015). "From predictive uplift modeling to prescriptive uplift analytics: A practical approach to treatment optimization while accounting for estimation risk." *Journal of Marketing Analytics* 3, no. 2, pp. 79–95.

MarketingSherpa. (2013). *2013 Email Marketing Benchmark Report*, Jacksonville Beach, FL: MECLABS.

CHAPTER 8

The Personalities of Email Users

Successful email campaigns are the result of knowing your audience. When do they open email? Do they read on mobile devices? In the previous chapters we have covered the basics of building and segmenting a list. Segments are built on the attributes of data that you collect. But there is another dimension that needs to be considered: What is the email personality of your audience?

The personality reveals a new dimension to the segment. Eli Langer, a producer for CNBC's social media team, recently posted a graphic on Twitter regarding email inboxes (see Figure 8.1).

Although this humorous email meme has appeared before, this was perhaps the first time it has generated a vigorous online discussion. However, what was interesting about this discussion was not that so many people offered explanations for the inbox with unread messages (e.g., laziness, popularity, bad email client, no knowledge of app badges) but rather that the notion of email user "types" clearly engaged and resonated with so many people.

Figure 8.1 *Types of inbox management*

Source: https://twitter.com/EliLanger/status/572081933452218368

Hoarder or Cleaner? Different Email User Typologies

So what do we know about different types of email users? Is there such a thing as an email style or personality? In a 2005 talk at PARC in Palo Alto, CA, Marissa Mayer said that Gmail designers discovered there were approximately six types of email users. Gmail was then designed around these six usage cases and tested within Google for two years prior to public announcement. This suggests that there may be more than two types of people in the email world, but Gmail's designers have never divulged their results; so we must look elsewhere to attempt to answer our questions. We will focus only on typologies rooted in empirical evidence (versus typologies based on the anecdotes or personal experiences of commentators).

One of the first typologies is due to Whittaker and Sidner (1996). These researchers conducted 1- to 2-hour interviews and gathered inbox statistics from 20 office workers using NotesMail at Lotus Development Corporation. Their analysis uncovered three types of users:

- Filers: People who file their messages every day
- Pilers: People who never file their messages
- Spring cleaners: Those who file once every 1 to 3 months

Though much has changed with email since 1996, Whittaker and Sidner's typology has held up well as a description of the basic way that email users differ in terms of email management. Dharmesh Mehta, senior director of Microsoft's Outlook.com, summarized his team's research in a 2013 interview with FastCompany.com by suggesting a user typology that is very similar to that of Whittaker and Sidner's. Specifically, he suggested that users tend to be one of three types:

- Filers: These users are very organized and use many techniques to maintain organization. "They have a lot of power tools to get through their Inbox and keep things where they want them," Mehta says.
- Pilers: They have thousands of things in their Inbox. Mehta suggests that pilers are users who may often have a sense of having missed something, "Like an important email, or something I forgot about, or something I was supposed to do."

- Deleters: Frequently start the day by deleting as many emails as they can. According to Mehta, roughly 50% of people ". . . take about a third of their Inbox and, before they even read the mail, they delete it."

MaCorr, an online marketing research company, recently used a slightly different approach to derive a typology. Rather than observing email behaviors and abstracting a set of user types, they predefined four user types and conducted a survey with 1,002 U.S. adults aged 18 to 65 who regularly use home and work email accounts. MaCorr asked people, "Please tell us which of the following four statements best describes your own 'email personality?' Consistent with Whittaker and Sidner (1996) and Mehta (2013), 95% of respondents identified themselves as typified by a focus on filing, piling (hoarding), or deleting.

- Deleter (55%): "You are conscientious and only keep an active inbox, deleting unnecessary emails and filing relevant ones. You respond to messages quickly and can be ruthless when deciding whether or not to reply."
- Filer (30%): "You regularly start email contact, and your emails are generally light hearted. Although you do not answer immediately you would not leave it more than one day. You deal with a lot of email so use inbox folders to keep conversations organized."
- Hoarder (10%): "You have a relaxed attitude to email. You rarely file or delete and don't pay too much attention to how your email tone might sound. You answer to emails only when you are ready."
- Printer (5%): "You print emails to read them and may also put them in paper files. You always reply with a prepared, considered response, so it could be that some emails aren't answered for a number of days. You are polite and traditional in tone and language."

Most recently, Kalman and Ravid (2015) revisited Whittaker and Sidner's (1996) seminal typology. They monitored the email accounts of 7,745 users for eight consecutive months, gathering data snapshots every hour (e.g., number of inbox messages, number of read messages, number of sent messages, average response time, and number of unread messages). This longitudinal analysis confirmed that although users do tend to exhibit a primary "type" that resembles piling, filing, and deleting, most users also periodically switched to alternative types to cope with accumulated effects or changes in email flows.

Managing Personal vs. Work Life

Email increasingly permeates our everyday lives through the evolution of new device affordances (Dery, Kolb, and MacCormick 2014). Grevet et al. (2014) found that whereas work email volume has doubled over time, personal email has increased five-fold (with particular gains in unread messages). Although new devices can enhance communication, they also present challenges in terms of greater email volume and greater expectations of "round-the-clock" responsiveness (Dearman and Pierce 2008). These issues highlight a key dimension along which people differ: work–life integration. At one end of the continuum, there is full integration of work and personal lives such that an individual has a single social existence with no boundaries between work and personal life. At the other end of the continuum, individuals treat work and life as completely separate existences. In reality, these endpoints represent extremes and most people fall somewhere in between, with periodic shifts toward one end to the other. Matthews et al. (2009) considered the role of different devices as well as different email accounts as boundary management artifacts, and found that email users tended to use their smartphones to remain aware of work developments and to perform "triage" on inboxes, but waited to read and respond to important emails on laptop or desktop computers.

Similarly, email often serves as a vehicle for "micro-role transitions" between work and life, such as when a worker receives an email from a spouse at work or when a worker receives an email from a colleague while at home (Ashforth, Kreiner, and Fugate 2000; Capra, Khanova, and Ramdeen 2013). Additional research suggests that work environments or cultures influence integration versus separation of work and personal lives. For example Cecchinato, Cox, and Bird (2015) examined a university setting and found that while both professional services staff and academics permitted work interruptions from personal emails, only academics allowed interruptions of personal lives with work emails. The authors also found that professional services staff restricted email on their phones to personal accounts, whereas academics used their phones for both personal and work accounts. Given that work–life conflict tends to induce stress, it is not surprising that people develop strategies to minimize transitions between work and home roles. Cecchinato, Cox, and Bird (2015) report examples that include (1) using the same device to check email but segregating work and personal emails by aligning them with separate applications (presumably to reduce the temptation of checking work/personal emails outside of work/personal roles), (b) disabling work email functionality from a phone when on leave or holiday, and (c) relying on dedicated folders and automated filtering for work and personal emails.

The Personality of Email Users

The notion of personality provides another way to think about why people perceive and use email in different ways (Reinke and Chamorro-Premuzic 2014; Whitbourne 2011). Personality is one of the oldest topics of study in social science, and is defined by the American Psychological Association as "individual differences in characteristic patterns of thinking, feeling, and behaving." Much evidence suggests that personality is largely a genetic disposition that takes similar forms across cultures but that there is early plasticity as individuals transact with their environments (John and Srivastava 1999; Livesley 2001; McCrae and Costa 2003; Woods and Roberts 2006).

The utility of personality is rooted in its ability to predict how people will behave in different situations. Additionally, recent advances in linguistics and computer science allow for accurate personality profiling based on text analyses of how people use sentiment words, parts of speech, grammar, punctuation, and other aspects of language and communication (e.g., Shen, Brdiczka, and Liu 2013; Wright and Chin 2014). This suggests two interesting possibilities: (1) Email marketers can garner important information on the personalities of their lists by simply analyzing responses to emails or other online expressions linkable by email (e.g., social media postings) and (2) email recipients are likely to infer the personalities of email marketers based on the content and construction of their emails. The practical implication is that email marketers should consider the extent to which the personality of their communications matches the personality of their recipients. Let us take a closer look at the structure of personality and then consider what it means for email marketers.

Although many conceptualizations have been proposed, the most influential and widely adopted perspective is that our personalities are comprised of five distinct and bipolar components: openness to experience, conscientiousness, extraversion, agreeableness, and neuroticism.

- *Openness to experience*: It involves curiosity, originality, insight, sensation seeking, and imagination, and includes a willingness to entertain a broad range of interests (e.g., exploring fantasies and adventure and appreciating the arts). High levels of openness to experience can manifest as delusional and unusual perceptions and beliefs about the world. Low levels of openness to experience may be expressed as particularly narrow or "black and white" thinking.
- *Conscientiousness*: It is characterized by high levels of thoughtfulness, goal-directed behavior, and good impulse control. Conscientious people tend to be attentive to detail, punctual, and reliable. High conscientiousness may be expressed as rigidity and perfectionism, whereas low conscientiousness manifests as recklessness and irresponsibility.
- *Extraversion*: An interpersonal disposition indicated by excitability, sociability, gregariousness, assertiveness, and willingness to self-disclose. Extroverts are often happy, talkative, expressive, and optimistic. High extraversion is associated with risky or intense reward seeking. Low extraversion manifests as extreme shyness, low interpersonal warmth, cautiousness, and impaired experience of positive emotions.
- *Agreeableness*: An interpersonal disposition characterized by trustworthiness, altruism, kindness, empathy, cooperativeness, and tender-mindedness. High levels of agreeableness may

appear as submissiveness, rejection-sensitivity, dependency, and indecisiveness. Low agreeableness can be expressed as entitlement, mistrust, callousness, and aggressiveness.

- *Neuroticism*: It is indicated by emotional instability, excessive worry, irritability, anxiety, self-doubt, and sadness. Neurotic individuals are pessimistic and tend to ruminate over their past failures. High levels of neuroticism are associated with low frustration tolerance, insecure attachment, emotional distress, and poor coping strategies. Low levels of neuroticism appear as emotional "flatness," even in stressful situations, as well as low-harm avoidance (i.e., lack of fear).

Our premise is that personality not only impacts how people use email technology and construct email messages but also what their preferences are likely to be in terms of receiving email content. Some examples are as follows:

- People who are higher in openness to experience will tend to be "pilers" and may be more receptive to novel or whimsical communications. In contrast, people who are lower in openness will tend to be "deleters" and may view novel or whimsical communications as flaky or purposeless.
- People who are higher in conscientiousness will tend to be "filers" and are likely to be more receptive to longer or detailed emails and are more critical of typos, grammatical errors, lapses in logic, or unclear intentions. People who are lower in conscientiousness will tend to be "pilers" and may be susceptible to risky propositions. They will also be unreliable partners in a marketing relationship.
- Extroverts will tend to be "pilers" who expect enthusiasm and energy (use exclamation points!) and will have a strong affinity for opportunities to express their opinions and inner feelings. People low in extroversion will tend to be "deleters" who eschew any efforts to arouse emotion or make "personal connections." They need to feel that communications are happening on their own terms.

- People who are higher in agreeableness will tend to be "filers" who will expect expressions of conviviality or intimacy, such as using personal salutations, saying "please," and expressing good wishes. People who are low in agreeableness will tend to be "deleters" who may be vocally unreceptive to email communications and other interpersonal "interruptions."

- Neurotic individuals will tend to be "filers," as they worry, overthink things, and keep close tabs on their environment for signs of problems or rejection. Communication with neurotics is fraught with danger since their anxieties and self-doubt cause them to find hidden meanings and aspersions in everything. They require constant and significant reassurances. People who are lower in neuroticism will tend to be "pilers" who may be difficult to offend but also difficult to engage due to their relatively flat emotional profile.

Exercise: Your Email Personality Test

Match your personality to your email behavior.

1. First, based on the definitions provided earlier, determine if you are a filer, piler, or deleter. (Hint: How many unopened emails are in your mail box?)
2. Next, read up on the formal definition of introversion and extraversion at http://psychologytoday.tests.psychtests.com/take_test.php?idRegTest=1311. Based on this description, how would you classify yourself? If you are unsure, use the Internet to search for a free self-test.
3. Now, how well do the descriptions in the last section match up with your email habits?
4. If you were marketing to yourself, what approach would you take in terms of schedule and number of emails given what you now know? Explain.

References

Ashforth, B., G. Kreiner, and M. Fugate. (2000). "All in a day's work: Boundaries and micro-role transitions." *Academy of Management Review* 25, no. 3, pp. 472–491.

Capra, R., J. Khanova, and S. Ramdeen. (2013). "Work and personal email use by university employees: PIM practices across domain boundaries," *Journal of the American Society for Information Science and Technology* 64, no. 5, pp. 1029–1044.

Cecchinato, M.E., A.L. Cox, and J. Bird. (2015). "Working 9–5? Professional differences in email and boundary management practices," *Proceedings of SIGCHI Conference on Human Factors in Computing Systems*, pp. 3989–3998. New York, NY: ACM Press.

Dearman, D. and J.S. Pierce. (2008). "It's on my other computer!: Computing with multiple devices," *Proceedings of SIGCHI Conference on Human Factors in Computing Systems*, pp. 767–776. New York, NY: ACM Press.

Dery, K., D. Kolb, and J. MacCormick. (2014). "Working with connective flow: How smartphone use is evolving in practice," *European Journal of Information Systems*, April, pp. 1–13.

Mehta, D. (2013). Interview with FastCompany (www.fastcompany .com/3014020/work-smart/whats-your-email-personality).

Grevet, C., D. Choi, D. Kumar, and E. Gilbert. (2014). Overload is overloaded!: Email in the age of Gmail," *Proceedings of SIGCHI Conference on Human Factors in Computing Systems*, pp. 793–802. New York, NY: ACM Press.

John, O.P. and S. Srivastava. (1999). "The Big Five trait taxonomy: History, measurment and theoretical perspectives." In *Handbook of Personality: Theory and Research*, eds. L.A. Pervin and O.P. John, (2nd edn), pp. 102–138. New York: Guilford Press.

Livesley, J.W. (2001). *Handbook of Personality Disorders: Theory, Research, and Treatment.* New York, NY: Guildford Press.

Kalman, Y.M., and G Ravid. (published online 2015). "Filing, piling, and everything in between: The dynamics of E-mail inbox management." *Journal of the Association for Information Science and Technology.* DOI: 10.1002/asi.23337

MaCorr. (2013). *Email Psychology Survey.* http://www.macorr.com /blog/?p=124, URL accessed October 8, 2015.

Matthews, T., J. Pierce, H. Road, S. Jose, and J. Tang. (2009). "No smart phone is an island: The impact of places, situation and other device on smart phone use." IBM Research Report, RJ10452 (A0909-003).

McCrae, R.R. and P.T. Costa. (2003). *Personality in Adulthood: A Five-Factor Theory Perspective* (2nd edn). New York, NY: Guilford Press.

Reinke, K. and T. Chamorro-Premuzic. (2014). "When email use gets out of control: Understanding the relationship between personality and email overload and their impact on burnout and work engagement." *Computers in Human Behavior* 36, no. July, pp. 502–509.

Shen, J., O. Brdiczka, and J. Liu. (2013). "Understanding email writers: Personality prediction from email messages." *Lecture Notes in Computer Science* 7899, pp. 318–330.

Whitbourne, S.K. (2011). "Using the Big 5 to diagnose your email personality," *Psychology Today,* July 25.

Whittaker, S. and C. Sidner. (1996). "Email overload: Exploring personal information management of email," *Proceedings of the SIGCHI Conference on Human Factors in Computing Systems,* pp. 276–283. New York, NY: ACM Press.

Woods, D. and B.W. Roberts. (2006). "Cross-sectional and longitudinal tests of the personality and role identity structural model (PRISM)." *Journal of Personality* 74, no. 3, pp. 779–810.

Wright, W.R. and D.N. Chin. (2014). "Personality profiling from text: Introducing part-of-speech N-grams." *Lecture Notes in Computer Science* 8538, pp. 243–253.

CHAPTER 9

Social Media and Email: Friend, Ally, or Frenemy?

With the rise of social media, many pundits trumpeted the old refrain that email is out of date and soon to perish. Yet, despite the rise in popularity of social media channels, email is still proving to be the most pervasive and effective method of directly marketing to and reaching customers. In their 2013 *National Client Email Report*, the Direct Marketing Association asserted that, "Email marketing remains critical to business, with 89% of respondents declaring email to be "important" or "very important" to their organization."

Why Is This?

First, email dominates social media in terms of usage. There are over 4 billion email addresses globally. About 75% of these addresses are consumer accounts. In contrast, Facebook has about 2.2 billion users, of which only 1.4 billion are considered active. As of this writing, LinkedIn has 322 million users and Twitter has 288 million users. Thus, there are 2 times more users of email than of Facebook and 10 times more users of email than of Twitter or LinkedIn. And to get started with any of these social media channels, you need to have an email address too.

Not only are there more consumer users of email, but also business users utilize their email more extensively than social media channels. Let us check a few facts:

- Facebook—average user spends 21 minutes a day[1]
- LinkedIn—only 40% of users check it once a day

---

[1] http://expandedramblings.com/index.php/by-the-numbers-17-amazing-facebook-stats/

- Twitter—29% check more than once a day; 46% use it at least once a day
- Email—business email users read 105 messages a day; 92% of adults are using it; 61% use it every day

Email is a critical and frequently used communication tool for business and nonbusiness users alike. Furthermore, when it comes to converting customers and generating revenue for businesses, email blows away social media. According to Custora's 2013 E-Commerce Customer Acquisition Snapshot (see Figure 9.1), organic search resulted in 16% of customer acquisition, while email accounted for roughly 7% of customer acquisition in Q2 2013. In contrast, social media channels resulted in less than 0.5% of customer acquisition. Additionally, email marketing shows the greatest growth in acquisition among all channels since 2010, whereas Facebook and Twitter have remained flat during the same period.

Social media also fails to stack up against email when considering customer lifetime value (CLV), or the net present value of expected future profits from a customer relationship. Facebook and Twitter acquisitions come in at 1% and -23%, relative to the average channel CLV. In contrast, customers acquired via email are worth 12% more than the average channel CLV (Custora 2013).

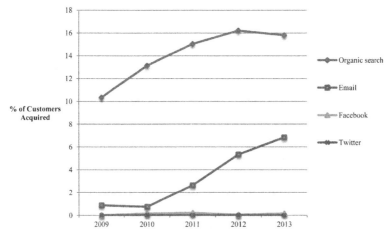

Figure 9.1 Growth of customer acquisition channels

Source: Custora's E-Commerce Customer Acquisition Snapshot, Q2 2013

Messaging in Social Media Platforms

Direct "email-like" messages are present in social media platforms. However, the social networks create barriers to using one-to-one and one-to-many direct messages for advertising.

- Facebook allows only users that are "friends" to message one another.
- LinkedIn allows unconnected people to connect with one another using "In Mail"—however, this is a single, user-to-user connection that should be used with discretion. It cannot be used for a business-to-user connection.
- Until 2015, Twitter allowed only direct messages if both people followed each other. Also, although Twitter allows you to create lists of people, you cannot bulk message these users.
- Text messages allow for the same sort of direct communication as email, but the limited character count makes it impractical. In addition, some consumers pay for individual text messages, so your business's advertising might be costing your customer. This practice is the equivalent of asking your customers to pay for the stamps for the postcards you mail them.

Social media messaging operates on the principle of both sides opting into a connection. And social media does not allow for the collection and creation of a list of users that can be bulk messaged like email.

What is a business to do? Social media requires businesses to think about how to entice users to connect with them—or opt-in—on social media by offering something of value. Even when a business successfully attracts followers to a social channel, it is never appropriate for the business to directly contact a follower through messages with an offer. This message would be quickly considered "spam" and generally a breach of social media etiquette. Such breaches of trust turn off customers rather than engage them.

So far, we have determined that email is used by more people, generates more revenue, and is more effective in reaching individual users. Social media offers direct messaging tools that resemble email, but these accounts cannot be gathered up to allow businesses to bulk message customers. Despite the continued and dominant effectiveness of email, it is obviously unwise to ignore social media channels in light of their impressive user growth rates.

Social Media and Email Are Fundamentally Different

Around 2010, marketing software companies and marketers anticipated a convergence between social media and email. Marketing automation and email platforms sought ways to add social media features into their applications and serve up reports of social media and email impacts in one unified dashboard. However, this convergence did not occur. In our experience with marketing groups at Fortune 500 companies, we did not see email marketing and social media marketing unify. Each channel was run by separate groups that often had little to no strategic overlap. Today, although social media and email may be closer in most organizations, they are recognized as unique and powerful in their own ways.

Let us take a look at how email and social media differ as communication channels. These differences require different styles of content and engagement models to be effective.

Email	Social Media
Direct communication	Broadcast communication
Private	Public
One-way communication	Two-way communication
Targeted to individual	Group
Segmentation by attributes	Relationships
Opt-in	Opt-in
Unaware of user's current state	Current state aware (Can reach out 1:1)
Planned	Immediate

Direct Communication vs. Broadcast Communication

Email targets an individual with a specific offer. It is the replacement for a postcard direct mailer or a newsletter sent to a home or business. Email and postal mail work on the same philosophy: gather a list of addresses and segment this list to allow for messages to be customized, to be more relevant to different "types" of recipients. Email has advantages over postal mail in that:

- *Email is cheaper*—There is no printing and no postage.
- *Email provides more data*—The marketer can tell what has been opened and what actions have been taken.
- *Email builds the list*—The actions taken from an email can be used to enrich the database and refine future segments.
- *Email is timely*—An email can be drafted and sent to respond to immediate situations or opportunities based on events, weather, or user activity.

In contrast, social media is a broadcast communication—news, content, or events are posted online and show up in the feeds of the users that have followed your organization or business. For organic social media, there is no way to reach out and target single users *en masse*.

Private Communication vs. Public Communication

Email is—in today's transparent world—relatively private in the sense that it is specifically targeted to a single person at their private account. (Of course, send something embarrassing, controversial or wrong, and an email may become very public when users post it on social media). In contrast, social media is public, broadcast communication. You post your business's content on social media channels and it will be viewed by any member of the social network who visits your page or profile. Unlike email, social media offers no way to track and target which *individuals* have viewed your social content. In email, you can see exactly which individuals opened messages and clicked to take action. This data is used to refine future email targeting. No such one-to-one passive data collection exists on social media. In social media you can tell in the aggregate how many times a post was viewed, but not which individuals viewed it.

One-Way Communication vs. Two-Way Communication

For business promotions, email is a one-way communication between the business and the consumer. Businesses do not expect consumers to write back, in the same way that you would never think about writing back after receiving a brochure in the mail. Ideally, social media is a two-way communication. If a customer reaches out on social media to your business, the customer's message and your business's response are public. This reaching out could be an @message to a company, a mention, or a comment on Facebook.

In this example, Jason mentioned JetBlue in a tweet. The JetBlue social media team jumped right on the opportunity to engage and thank him for his business. Social media is allowing JetBlue to have a one-to-one interaction. It is not a sales pitch. They do not offer a credit card or try to sell him an upgrade. They simply thank him and let the conversation continue. JetBlue is using Twitter to build rapport. This channel and interaction was important, because 10 minutes later he had a customer service problem.

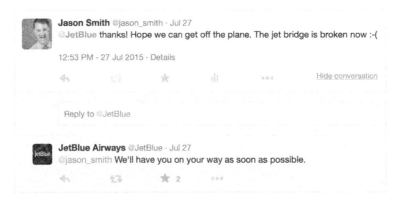

The social media team is doing a good job by responding quickly—less than 2 minutes—and apologizing for the delay. The next day Jason received a $25 credit in my email. Social media allowed JetBlue to build a one-to-one relationship, provide customer support, and offered an opportunity to follow and make right a service lapse.

Segmentation vs. Relationship

Bulk business-driven emails are found on a massive database of email addresses and attributes. As we presented in Chapter 6, with email, marketers often segment or divide the users based on different attributes. They then target different content to the relevant email addresses. Segmentation attributes might include the following:

- Demographics: age, gender, ethnicity, household income
- Product interest categories
- Interactions: opens, clicks, time of day
- Buying habits: time of month, average product
- Company relationship: loyalty member, coupon user

Through data analysis, a marketing team may identify segments of users based on combinations of attributes. Some example segments might include the following:

- Female, 25 to 35, mom, coupon user
- Male, 55to 65, sale purchase, retired, top 10% purchaser

Based on these segments, the marketing team generates email offers and sends them off to these customers. As users interact with these emails and make more purchases, more data is added to the database that can be used to refine future emails.

None of this data mining exists in *organic* social media. The ability to segment users and target a specific user is just not possible. Social media is broadcasting out a message to all of the customers that you are connected with. Some businesses pursue some *very* rudimentary segmentation by creating different social media channels. JetBlue offers a regular Twitter account and a Twitter account for special offers.

Notice, we said segmentation does not happen in *organic* social media. (Organic social media is social media that you have not paid for.) One of the things that make social media so compelling to marketers is the potential to use all of the personal information that social media users willingly provide to target advertising. Facebook becomes the database of personal information full of rich attributes—likes, dislikes, friends, hometown, workplace, college, year of graduation, favorite TV shows, music, products, relationship status—that marketers can use to show ads.

Opt-In and Opt-In

Yes, that is right—both social media and email need to be opt-in. To make these channels most effective (and to follow the law for email), you need to generate value for customers and let them choose to receive your content. This value could be something funny, informational, or an offer. For social media, this means getting customers to like or follow your company; in other words, you need to get a customer to want to receive your content in their feeds. For email, you need to get customers to willingly provide their email so that you may communicate with them directly through their inbox.

Current State Aware

Email is a one-way communication that relies on past behaviors to establish relevance. Social media happens in real time. Companies can communicate directly with customers via social media and also engage them with offers. In our work, we have seen some clients look to use big data to mine social media for product interest—e.g., "I'm looking to buy a car" or "I'm planning a trip to Florida"—and then target messages via social media or email. Automating this process is not in reach for most businesses.

Planned vs. Immediate

In general, as we are thinking about email, it is planned. You take your email list, you segment it, you generate the segment list, you create offers for the segment, and you send the email to the list. Social media can be much more immediate. The now famous Oreo tweet from the 2013 SuperBowl is a great example. When the power went out during the game, Oreo's social media team quickly whipped up this tweet:

This tweet connected with users because it was immediate and commenting on a broadly shared experience during a major cultural event. This tweet is just a quick, timely twist on an existing strategy. The Twitter strategy for Oreo features content about dunking. The real-time response leveraged an existing strategy, creative and brand message, and took the campaign to the next level.

Using Social Media to Build Your Email List

OK, social media and email are different and have different purposes. How can they work together?

A B2B business can use social media to promote thought-leadership. First, the business needs to build social media channels with potential customers as followers. Second, to effectively use this tactic, the business generates high-quality, customer-centered content that can be published at their website. It is critical that the content be educational, informative, and valuable to potential or current customers. In other words, the content should not be a press release, product sales sheet, or a direct offer. Social media can then be used to promote this content to followers. Each social media post should link back to the website. Once at the website, the business should provide an opportunity for the prospect to sign up to receive by email more valuable content (like the piece she is currently reading).

This social to email strategy will also work for a consumer package goods (CPG) company. If the company gains a strong social following, the CPG company can post out editorial content or offers such as coupons on social media. These links again should return followers to the website to read the content. The site should offer a call-to-action to sign up for a newsletter. For coupons, the coupons should offer a valuable carrot for customers to provide their email and to opt-in to future offers.

What Comes after Social Media? Proximity Marketing

At the start of this chapter, we made the statement that email is generally the most efficient and effective way to send a direct message to a customer. A new and potentially interesting variation on this theme is "proximity marketing." This type of marketing allows businesses to push messages to your mobile device when you are within a certain perimeter by using Bluetooth through a beacon device. This technology allows companies to send a direct message to you simply because you have approached or entered a store or are traversing a specified location within the store (e.g., the jeans section). Based on your location you can receive a targeted message. At this point, this message is based solely on your proximity to a beacon device as well as the fact that you have mobile device with a receiving app. Examples of proximity marketing can be found in Apple retail stores as well as in stores of national chains such as Ann Taylor and Urban Outfitters.

Best Practices for Leveraging Content for Email and Social Media

When developing outbound-marketing content, many organizations think about the principle of COPE: Create Once, Publish Everywhere. This means creating one core piece of content and pushing it out across all of the different channels. What is important to note is that this is not *write* once, it is *create* once. Each piece is created once but it needs to be promoted (written) differently on different channels.

For example, if you create an article for your consulting business, you do not want to just tweet out the title or publish the entire article via email.

- *Unique tweets and posts*—Do not just use the title, "Read my new article on XYZ." Rather, find something from the article that is shareable and valuable. Think of good tweets as good pull quotes from a magazine article.
- *Use images*—When posting on social media, using images can increase engagement with a message dramatically. According to a March 2014 study conducted by Socialbakers.com, over 75% of the content posted on Facebook was photography. Similarly, using an image on Twitter increases retweets by 35%. An image does not need to be a photograph—it can be a chart, graph, nicely typeset

quote, or a photograph. Social media is a visual media and humans are adept visual processors. If you want engagement, it is difficult to beat images as a technique for drawing people into your content.

- *Promoting content via email*—When you promote your content via email do not email the entire article. You should write a good summary using bullet points and subheads. Pitch the article to your audience telling them why the content is valuable.

- *YouTube*—YouTube can be used in many different ways to promote content. For example, it is relatively easy to produce a short, 10-second video that teases a piece of content. This can be shared socially or added to a website or embedded in an email. It may also be worthwhile to produce a series of narrated slides that introduce the content. Note also that YouTube represents an opportunity for search engine optimization (SEO)—carefully consider the title and the description you give your video to maximize search engine impact.

- *Slideshare*—Take the key points from your article and put them into a slide deck and share it on www.slideshare.net. This will provide users another way to access your content, plus it will improve your SEO.

Exercise

- Select three organizations or businesses that you are receiving promotional email from already: try to select them from different categories. For example:
  - A large company—Macy's, Sports Authority, CVS
  - A small business or single product company—perhaps a software package, airline, or travel company
  - A professional service, thought-leader, or nonprofit—accounting, law firm, or content channel like MarketingProfs

- Follow these businesses on different social media channels (Facebook, Instagram, LinkedIn, and Twitter):
  - Over a week, compare the content in email and social media messages.
    - How is the tone different?
    - Are the messages in email and social media coordinated?
    - How are they using images, graphics, or text?
    - Where does content from social media link to—the corporate website, microsite, or blog?
  - Observe ways that they are trying to build their email list or gather additional personal information.

Reference

CUSTORA. E-Commerce Customer Acquisition Snapshot | Q2 2013

The Direct Marketing Association. (2013). "National client email report" (www.dma.org.uk/research/national-client-email-report-2013 accessed July 2015).

CHAPTER 10

Integrating Email with Big Data

In Steven Spielberg's 2002 futurist thriller *Minority Report*, we see Tom Cruise frantically walking through a mall attempting to avoid recognition and capture. As he pushes past the crowds, the multimedia animated ads call out to him by name beckoning him to take a vacation, drink a Guinness, or buy a new Lexus. Upon entering the Gap, a holographic greeter welcomes him by name and asks how: "How did the tank tops work out for you?" As he wanders through the store, we hear the greeter ask every new customer how they enjoyed their previous purchases, in a perky, enthusiastic tone clearly aimed at enticing customers into more purchases. The movie imagines a retina-scanning device to identify each person uniquely, a technology that takes a humorous bent when the character has his eyes surgically swapped to remain anonymous and hide his identity.

These scenes highlight how marketers are always looking for ways to make increasingly real-time and one-to-one connections with customers. In addition, they show a future where the lines between digital, data, and physical spaces are blurred.

Today, we rely on an email address rather than on retina scans to establish the unique identity, but companies are starting to use the troves of data they have about customers to provide more accurate and real-time messages, experiences, or offers. This next evolution of email marketing (and marketing in general) is omnichannel campaigns: presenting the right message to the right customer at the right time regardless of location or device. And we will see a move beyond email becoming the unique identifier as wireless devices—phones and watches today—become more integrated into our lives. Omnichannel will begin to connect your email, your purchase history, and your phone or other wireless device to influence your purchases or provide a more customized experience.

To execute on omnichannel marketing campaigns, companies and organizations need to centralize and make available all of their data in a single repository or warehouse and then perform large-scale data analysis to find more discreet segments. That is to say, they need a big data solution.

First What Is Big Data?

Big data is the concept of collecting large data sets and then analyzing these big data sets to find patterns or trends. It may be helpful to think of Big Data as a process to analyze data from a variety of sources in different structures from many locations (Weinberg, Davis, & Berger 2013). For marketers, the goal of this analysis is to develop more meaningful segments based on interaction and behavior. As we have discussed throughout this book, email marketing (and marketing in general) has always been about collecting data, analyzing data, creating segments, and sending out more targeted messages. Big data offers the opportunity to do this type of complex analysis on much, much larger data sets with much more complex analysis. The promise is the ability to create increasingly smaller segments and personalized messages that are based on data.

Before Big Data

Before big data, this customer data existed in silos and legacy systems that did not communicate with each other, and the tools to process and analyze this data into meaningful, actionable information were scarce.

Let us look at all of the data that a retailer may have (see Figure 10.1):

- Online Store—customer accounts, purchase history, preferences, browsing history, credit cards
- Coupon Engine—customer account, coupon preference, redemption activity
- In-Store Point of Sale system—purchase history
- Marketing CRM—email address, website activity, segmentations, contact information, direct mail history
- Rewards program—enrollment, usage, history, special offers

Figure 10.1 Data warehouse structure

The first step to leverage big data is to create or purchase a solution to feed all of this information into one location. The second step is to connect a customer's data in from one system to another. To make this link happen, the systems need unique identifiers to connect these different data sources. A unique identifier could be a name, street address and zip code, or an email address. Although email is frequently used because it is by default unique, there may be challenges in that multiple people—most typically a couple—may use the same credit card, email address, or rewards profile making the profile data imperfect. The third step is to analyze all of these data to find new segments, new trends, and new patterns. Once these patterns are identified, then new campaigns can be created to reach out these customers with increased precision.

A Brand without Big Data

When you take most product brands—diapers, yogurt, dish detergent—you will see on the brand website they are looking to build a relationship with consumers directly and encourage them to purchase more product, without selling it directly. The brands are building social channels and an email list with value-added content, and they are offering coupons, special offers, and promoting charity programs to drive more sales and build brand equity. In many cases, the email sign-ups and coupon sign-ups are handled by two different systems—a CRM and a third-party coupon provider (see Figure 10.2).

Marketers send out emails via the CRM and they can measure opens, click-through rates, and content performance. They can even tell which customers follow the links to the web-based coupons. But, the CRM does not track whether the user downloaded coupons, which coupons were downloaded, or where and when the coupons are used. Customer selection and downloads of coupons is often tracked in a third-party outsourced system (these systems are cheaper and already integrated with the stores). Determining if the coupon was redeemed in a store also requires the third-party vendor to partner with point of sale (POS) systems.

So, before data integration, each system captures data about the user, but this data remains trapped inside the system and it cannot be merged with other data and leveraged to create more targeted campaigns in the future.

The data flow is one way. Data is trapped in each system. In the future state, the data from each system is collected and passed back to the previous system or into a large centralized data warehouse for analysis.

When the data integration state exists (see Figure 10.3), the marketing CRM has a whole new set of attributes—product interest, coupon interest, purchase history, and so on—to enhance segments for email marketing.

No Data Integration

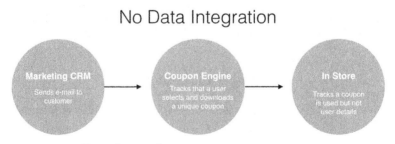

Figure 10.2 Data flow without integration

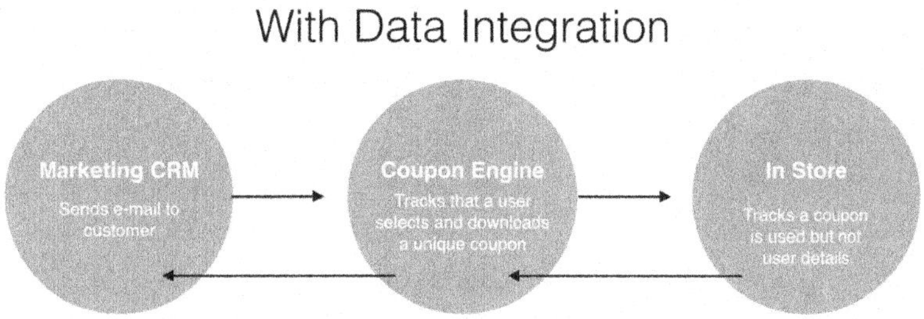

With Data Integration

Figure 10.3 Data flow with integration

Using Big Data in Email

The promise of aggregating all of these data into one warehouse is that the business will be able to use all of the data to close the loop on the marketing activities. Let us look at how a big data approach could help an email program:

- An email promoting specific products results in a confirmed in-store purchase of these products. Further analysis would reveal the halo effect of this email showing not only that a specific product was purchased, but also what other items were sold.

- Leverage rewards data to enhance segmentation and better tailor messages in an email. This could include calls to action to use rewards points. The email could include specific account balances. Seasonality of purchases can be used to better target emails as well.

There is one level of integration that allows for transactions to take place and another level that allows for the proactive marketing to happen. On the transactional level, retail businesses need to integrate their stores' physical inventory and purchasing process with their online inventory and purchasing process to allow consumers to browse the content via the website and see if it is available in their local store or to make a purchase online and return the product at a local store.

On a marketing level, the data from all of these different systems need to be pooled into one data repository or warehouse so that it can be analyzed and leveraged for marketing purposes in all channels— email, in-store, ecommerce or mobile app. With centralized data markets can do the following:

- Use in-store purchase history to make recommendations in the mobile app or in the online store
- Use online browsing behavior to personalize the mobile app to show you specials that are relevant

From an email opportunity, with big data retailers are able to leverage in-store habits and buying patterns with online activity.

- Personalize the mobile app when the user checks into the store with recently viewed items online
- Earn bonus or reward points online or in the store
- Use in-store purchases to augment the online profile to allow for more targeted emails and online recommendations

Ultimately, mobile devices will be able to track your information, share it back to the CRM, and allow the business to use this ultimately to trigger another email to you with even more accuracy.

Using Other Data Sources

Big data does not just need to be your data; it can be any data that you can capture. Big data is becoming a big idea and reality as the cost of computing infrastructure available decreases. Now that companies can easily buy massive amounts of storage in the cloud for pennies and on-demand, it is less and less expensive to capture data and perform analysis against these huge data sets.

How else might big data work to help email? Imagine ingesting all of the Twitter data—every single tweet, every day—and performing data analysis on this massive data set to find patterns relevant to your business: people looking to purchase a car, a new home, or attending a sporting event. If these users or patterns can be identified, then messages can be targeted to these people. And if the Twitter account can be linked to an email in your customer database, suddenly your customer profiles are richer and more real time than ever. You could target these users with information about your product via email.

Reference

Weinberg, B.D., L. Davis, and P.D. Berger. (2013). "Perspectives on Big Data." *Journal of Marketing Analytics* 1, no. 4, pp. 187–201.

Index

OTHER TITLES IN OUR DIGITAL AND SOCIAL MEDIA MARKETING AND ADVERTISING COLLECTION

Vicky Crittenden, Babson College, Editors

- *Viral Marketing and Social Networks* by Maria Petrescu
- *Herding Cats: A Strategic Approach to Social Media Marketing* by Andrew Rohm and Michael Weiss
- *Social Roots: Why Social Innovations Are Creating the Influence Economy* by Cindy Gordon, John P. Girard, and Andrew Weir
- *Social Media Branding For Small Business: The 5-Sources Model* by Robert Davis
- *A Beginner's Guide to Mobile Marketing* by Karen Mishra and Molly Garris
- *Social Content Marketing for Entrepreneurs* by James M. Barry
- *Digital Privacy in the Marketplace: Perspectives on the Information Exchange* by George Milne
- *This Note's For You: Popular Music + Advertising = Marketing Excellence* by David Allan
- *Digital Marketing Management: A Handbook for the Current (or Future) CEO* by Debra Zahay
- *Corporate Branding in Facebook Fan Pages: Ideas for Improving Your Brand Value* by Eliane Pereira Zamith Brito, Maria Carolina Zanette, Carla Caires Abdalla, Benjamin Rosenthal, and Mateus Ferreira
- *Presentation Skills: Educate, Inspire and Engage Your Audience* by Michael Weiss
- *The Connected Consumer* by Dinesh Kumar

Announcing the Business Expert Press Digital Library

Concise e-books business students need for classroom and research

This book can also be purchased in an e-book collection by your library as

- a one-time purchase,
- that is owned forever,
- allows for simultaneous readers,
- has no restrictions on printing, and
- can be downloaded as PDFs from within the library community.

Our digital library collections are a great solution to beat the rising cost of textbooks. E-books can be loaded into their course management systems or onto students' e-book readers. The **Business Expert Press** digital libraries are very affordable, with no obligation to buy in future years. For more information, please visit www.businessexpertpress.com/librarians. To set up a trial in the United States, please email **sales@businessexpertpress.com.**

0 1341 1661958 3

CPSIA information can be obtained at www.ICGtesting.com
Printed in the USA
BVOW06s1654140516

447938BV00005B/27/P

9 781606 499924